A
Cheshire
Christmas

A
Cheshire
Christmas

Compiled by Alan Brack

ALAN SUTTON PUBLISHING LIMITED

First published in the United Kingdom in 1994
Alan Sutton Publishing Limited · Phoenix Mill · Far Thrupp
Stroud · Gloucestershire

First published in the United States of America in 1994
Alan Sutton Publishing Inc. · 83 Washington Street · Dover
NH 03820

British Library Cataloguing in Publication Data

ISBN 0-7509-0553-0

Library of Congress Cataloging in Publication Data
applied for

Cover illustration: detail from Schoolchildren playing in the
snow, *by Johan Mari ten Kate (1831–1910). (Reproduction
courtesy of Fine Art Photographic Library, London.)*

Typeset in Garamond 12/13.
Typesetting and origination by
Alan Sutton Publishing Limited.
Printed in Great Britain by
WBC, Bridgend, Mid Glam.

Contents

A Cheshire Christmas

A Cheshire Christmas

A Cheshire Christmas

From the Moment the Turkeys Arrive . . .

GAIL COOPER

Gail Cooper is an award-winning journalist and broadcaster who was born in Wirral and educated at West Kirby Grammar School. She is a former editor of the Hoylake and West Kirby News *and the* Wirral News. *Although far from being disaffected with life in the Wirral peninsula, she and her businessman husband Graham (also Wirral-born) had long yearned for a place in the country where they could lead 'The Good Life'. In 1985 they took the plunge. Within a week of seeing it advertised they had bought an idyllically situated smallholding in the beautiful Vale of Clwyd.*

Gail is still a full-time journalist and Graham is still in business but their 30-acre smallholding with its flock of Jacob's sheep, its ducks, geese and hens and Tara, a handsome if rather haughty chestnut mare and Jane, her sooty-black donkey companion, is a constant joy to come home to.

But it all means hard work – very hard work – and Christmas for them starts early.

Christmas on the smallholding starts in August. From the moment the four-week-old Cheshire turkeys arrive, neurotically pale and piping, we're under starter's orders.

During the next four months they will change and grow from puny specimens into magnificent birds to grace the Christmas table. The countryside must seem wild and frightening to them at first, despite the snug Victorian stable prepared for them. Until now home has been a modern building where food, light, heat and water are electronically controlled and delivered. Here a fat cat straddles the wall between their stable and the next, ready to pounce from above on an unsuspecting mouse like the wrath of God. Beyond the wall live two fine cockerels, competing for crowing honours. One is dressed in flaming autumn golds and reds, the other barred and dappled in black and white, mysteriously lacking his tail feathers. Up the hill, sheep graze, chickens scratch, and a horse and donkey bicker companionably.

As autumn follows on from summer, the turkeys flourish. The boldest birds take to the air, perching on wall or stable door to sun themselves in the September breeze. On fine days the door is propped open so the turkeys can explore the gravelled yard. They inspect the neighbouring ducks with interest and flee like terrified virgins before the fierce white geese, armed with huge beaks and powerful wings.

They experience the real country night: velvet-black and star-spangled, punctuated by strange cries and rustles. Tucked up in their stable, the turkeys sleep, but jerk nervously into wakefulness to pipe their strange cry in echo of a hunter's triumphant call. A disturbed pheasant clatters anxiously on its hedgerow perch, as owl and fox begin their nightly rounds.

Autumn must be the best season on the smallholding, although spring, with its promise and hope, runs a close second. In autumn an Indian summer brings warm and sunny

days, crisp frosts to cleanse the soil and leave a magic morning tracery on every blade and bush.

October is the month for completing the harvest begun so frantically in September. The greenhouse tomatoes are stripped of fruit and endless vats of soup or sauce bubble on the Rayburn, fired up again and welcoming after its summer rest.

The hedgerows yield glossy elderberries, sloes with blue-black bloom, rosy crab apples and the last of the blackberries. Jams and jellies are made and stored for Christmas. There is wood to be brought down for the crackling fires which leap in the open hearth as darkness falls.

In their stable, the turkeys are growing strong and sturdy. While their deep-litter counterparts on factory farms are putting on flesh at the expense of bone to support them, these birds grow more naturally.

The earliest of the turkey customers puts in a repeat order for her bird in January. But by October the serious list is hanging on the kitchen wall. One friend is entertaining sixteen for Christmas lunch and wants a huge bird; another wants a more modest 12-pounder. Hard to explain to supermarket-trained shoppers that nature operates a lottery; some birds will be bigger than others among our twenty-five.

In November the short days and long nights mean that every bright hour is a bonus which helps the birds grow. Greedy for food and water now, they recognise our footsteps and clamour for attention when we fill the coal scuttle nearby.

Occasionally one bird gets out and spends the day investigating plant pots and water barrels, piping in its fluty voice at any strange sound. Shepherded back in, its Colditz tendencies are hampered by an artful arrangement of old brooms and garden rakes across the stable door.

The day on which Christmas falls is important to the small turkey grower. Birds need to be killed a week to ten days

before they are eaten to allow for maximum hanging after death and the development of that real turkey flavour. European Community 'hygiene police' tried to ban this practice which for centuries has produced perfect and beautiful meat but, happily, howls of protest made them give way.

The killing is done by an old countryman who remembers despatching his first bird when he was just nine. A modern building is hung with plastic like an operating theatre and the team of three men – two of them pluckers – don gauze masks, for tiny underfeathers and turkey dander can cause wheezy chests. It's never made clear why but a bottle of whisky is a vital component of the equipment, too.

Not for these birds an agonising journey by lorry, crushed and broken, exposed to the elements, on their way to death. Nor do they face the hideous electronic stunning carousel. The few steps from stable to killing room are accomplished in moments; the merciful knife is plunged speedily, and the struggling bird is pinioned in its death throes. Within seconds the bird is cooling to a piece of meat and the pluckers get rapidly to work.

We pray for hard frost and chilly days in the crucial week before Christmas. The plucked birds are hung, still ungutted, to mature. Then the rush really starts as twenty-five birds need to be cleaned and trussed, and every customer demands delivery at the same time.

That holiday feeling starts for us as the last cardboard box with its meaty burden is despatched, and the finest specimen is crammed into our own fridge.

Herbs from the garden, quick-frozen in September, perfume the stuffing on Christmas Eve as the fruits of our labour are brought out to be admired by the house party. Sloe gin, rich as purple silk, is sipped, mince pies are warmed, and the expectation of another Christmas Day builds up.

Cutting Christmas trees in Delamere Forest for Christmas 1963

In the stable, the horse and donkey exude warm breath smelling of hay, and whicker to us as we creep out. It is midnight on Christmas Eve and legend has it that we will find them on their knees, ready to speak in human tongue, praising that most holy of days in the Christian calendar.

Will they talk tonight? In this magical valley, by Christmas starlight, it is easy to believe they will.

Run-up to Christmas

DORA KENNEDY

Early in November comes the flood
of catalogues; packets of Christmas cards,
pamphlets of hampers, turkeys, cut-price wine –
exotic gifts of intricate design,
and, like a grey note in a merry song,
the cry of Third World children drifts along.

School concerts, draws, tickets of every hue
for cakes, dressed dolls, a fortnight in Corfu.
Packed pavements, carols (canned) on strident waves;
bewildered children tour Aladdin caves
are lost, and found, still in a magic dream;
yet this is just the background, not the theme.

Last-minute shopping, how the money flows,
six kinds of cheese; now why did we buy those?
Beds aired, erected, one leg falters still;
tables to set and stockings yet to fill.
Gilt, glitter, mistletoe and candle light –
froth on the surface of this wondrous night.

The midnight Church, tall taper's solemn glow.
Stars in the sky, frail peace on earth below.
This is the heart of it, the very core,
Hope, within a manger, born once more.

The Chester Christmas Watch

The last time any citizens of Chester were called upon to keep a night watch over their city was just over fifty years ago when the threat of attack came from the German Air Force. But the first time was 900 years before that – and at Christmas.

Soon after Hugh Lupus had established himself in the city as the first Earl of Chester it was invaded one Christmas Eve by a fierce band of Welshmen who, unlike their latter-day descendants, had not come for the shopping.

It has been suggested that the raiders may well have been a mixed force of Welshmen, Saxons and Britons living over the border and hostile to the Normans. But whoever they were they took the city by surprise and much blood was shed in the fighting that followed. When the attackers eventually withdrew over the border they left a large part of Chester in flames.

The Reverend Robert Rogers, writing in the sixteenth century in the free-style spelling of those days, gave a graphic

account of the raid, based, as he pointed out, on the writings of past historians:

> No man's memorie cannot remember the origenal, yet the collections of writers doe shew the beginning to be in the dayes of William the Conqueror, who driving the oulde Brittons, or as is verylye thoughte the Walshemen who did here inhabitt, mixed with the oulde Saxons, seeing the Normans to have gotten the possession by force of conquest, at a season in the Christmas when all men give themselves to securitie, the Walshemen, neere neighbours, grudgeing at their securitie and possession of their landes came in the nighte time and made a sudden invasion, and spoiled and burned some of this cittie.

Hugh Lupus was determined that the city would not be caught unawares again. For a start he gave land to families who, in return, would provide armies of retainers for 'Watching the Four Gates'. The appointed tenants also paid a 'gabel' (a tax) every Christmas. In default of payment the tenant faced a fine and the forfeiture of his land to the king.

This special Christmas watch on the walls was kept up for centuries but in later times it was not mounted because of fear of attack by disgruntled Welshmen so much as the fear of vandalism, arson and theft by roistering citizens, as the Reverend Rogers pointed out:

> The use that now is made thereof is . . . to watch 3 nightes together with the most strong and well-appointed armore . . . but now we use the same to kepe the cittie from danger of fire, theeves, dronkness, and unmeete meetings and drinkinges in the nightes, which might be the cause of perturbations of peace and sin against God, which to these times are most incidente . . .

Over the years Setting of the Watch became a great annual ceremony and signalled the beginning of the City of Chester's Christmas celebrations.

On Christmas Eve the Mayor and Corporation, with the Court of Aldermen, Justices of the Peace, Recorder and other important personages sat formally at the Common Hall to Set the Watch. The tenants were called by proclamation to render homage for their lands and the men-at-arms were inspected before parading through the streets with banners flying to the four gates. And, it almost goes without saying, the procedure was followed by a banquet.

On record is a letter dated 17 December 1667, from the then Mayor, Richard Harrison, to Sir William Williams, the new Recorder of Chester (and a forebear of the well-known Williams Wynn family) explaining what would be expected of him on this traditional occasion and formally inviting him to be present and take part:

Sir,

It has beene an ancient custome of this Cittie yearly upon Christmas Eve, that the Justices of the Peace, Aldermen and Com'on Councell meet at the Maior's house about six o'clock that evening; and then the Maior, Recorder and Justices . . . in their scarlett gownes, attended with lights and torches and accompanied with diverse of the gentry and others, goe thence to the Co'en Hall. And beeing sate there (where is usually a great concourse of people). Silence beeing com'anded, the Customary Tenants of the Cittie, are then called to doe their services; who, by persons for them, appear in armes to watch and guard the Cittie for that night.

Then the Recorder makes a Speech declaring the occasion of that meeting, the venerable antiquitie of the Cittie . . . the keyes of the Cittie gates are delivered up

Skates or no skates, ice-hockey was the game when Pickmere froze
over around the turn of the century

to the Maior and by him delivered to such of the
watchmen as he is pleased to intrust. . . Then the Maior,
Recorder, Justices (etc.) returne to the Maior's house. . .
And, after a collation . . . depart . . .

Wherefore I thought fitt to give you the trouble of this
relac'on . . . to be informed whether . . . your occasions
. . . will afford us your presence here . . . At the request of
Yo'r affectionate freind
Richard Harrison, Maior.

And, no doubt, a gudde tyme was hadde bye alle.

from

Green and Pleasant Land

NORMAN MURSELL

Norman Mursell spent his entire working life as a gamekeeper on the Eaton Estate, serving five Dukes of Westminster in succession. He told his story in his book Come Dawn, Come Dusk *and so successful was it that he returned to his desk to write* Green and Pleasant Land, *a diverting record of his life in and around Eaton, near Chester, during the years leading up to and immediately after the Second World War.*
Most of his career was spent in the service of the famous Croesus-rich second duke (better known as 'Bendor') whose seat, Eaton Hall, was nothing less than a vast Gothic Revival palace from where he led a life of unparalleled luxury and extravagance.

In the second duke's day several chauffeurs were employed and when a large number of guests were due to arrive at Chester or Crewe stations a local taxi firm would have two or three cars based at Eaton, ready to be called upon day or night. This must have been a very welcome source of income for the Chester taxis, with the meter ticking away for twenty-four hours at a time.

I recall one incident in which a taxi was concerned. For once the second duke was spending Christmas at Eaton, and there was quite a houseparty in residence. A two-day shoot had taken place on 22 and 23 December, and most guests were stopping over for the festive season. The gamekeepers had the almost impossible task of disposing of over two thousand pheasants which had been shot. The gift list was a long one and to ensure that the larder was cleared before Christmas, an estate lorry was called into service and a taxi was allocated to the game department to deal with the distribution of the birds. I was appointed to go with the taxi and take a brace of pheasants here, a brace of pheasants there. A large number had to be distributed in Chester itself and a taxi driver was the right man to find his way about the city.

It was mid-morning on the 24th before the lists were sorted out and the pheasants labelled, so after a quick coffee in the servants' hall a start was made on the tour of Chester. Christmas Eve has always been a busy time in any town or city and Chester is no exception. There were pheasants for the Bishop of Chester, the Mayor, the Chief Constable and other senior officers, the manager of the Grosvenor Hotel, the stationmaster and even one particular ticket-collector, and many other fortunate folk. With the heavy traffic, and even in those days some parking problems, it was early afternoon when the task was completed.

On arriving back at Eaton, the taxi was met by Fred Milton, the head gamekeeper, who had another load ready and labelled and these birds were to be delivered to various people over a large area of Cheshire! It was rather late for lunch but a snack was soon rustled up by the kitchen staff before the taxi once more set off on its rounds. Although there weren't as many brace of pheasants in this load, the distance to be covered was much greater, so care had to be taken over the route to ensure that we did not retrace our steps. After travelling many miles

and making many enquiries for directions on the largely unfamiliar territory, I finally delivered the last brace of pheasants in Crewe, some twenty-odd miles from Chester. At this point Arthur, the taxi driver, suddenly remembered that he hadn't collected his own Christmas dinner, a large joint of pork, which had been ordered from a butcher's in Chester! Arthur decided to call at home with the meat in case his wife was getting anxious about its, and his, whereabouts before taking me back to Eaton. It was by now seven o'clock in the evening so a cup of tea and a piece of cake provided by 'Mrs Arthur' were most welcome. Thinking the day's work was completed we took our refreshment at leisure. Hard luck – it was not so! On our arrival back at Eaton who should immediately appear but Albert Hopkins, the duke's valet. 'I'm sorry,' he said, 'but here are some Christmas cards. His Grace wants them delivering at once. I'm afraid you're the only transport free. Will you see to it?'

Of course there wasn't any option really, but on examining the wad of cards I discovered that a large part of the area covered that afternoon had to be travelled again! Petrol in the tank of the taxi was getting low so the first stop was Arthur's depot to refill – no all-night filling stations in those days. Then off we went on the postman's run till about 11.30 that evening; only one card was left, for the district nurse in the village of Tattenhall. Fortunately the first person we asked knew the nurse's residence so a tired Arthur said, 'Thank God. Let's get back to Eaton'. Albert, the valet, was still up when we got back – a good many of the staff did not dare go to bed until the duke did and Albert was no exception. He was very pleased that the Christmas cards had all been delivered since the duke had asked several times during the evening about them. A good stiff whisky was now in order and as Arthur was about to depart he was given a bottle of the 'mountain dew' with the compliments of His Grace.

This was a most unusual incident for Bendor seldom put pen to paper, let alone sent out Christmas cards, but on this occasion although the envelopes were typed the cards bore the duke's signature. Some of those cards could still be treasured by families somewhere in Cheshire.

All on Twopence a Week

The joys and disappointments of Christmas in a Cheshire village in the 1920s

MARY NICHOLLS

In those past days no-one ever thought of Christmas until the Collect for the last Sunday after Trinity with its rousing 'Stir up' reminded Mother of mincemeat. The following day we visited the butcher. Suet was then the real stuff, cut straight from the beast, and none of your packet mysteries as it is today. We flinched as Mr Ingham brandished his terrible knife, and cut exactly the amount required. This had to be shredded at home before use.

Our next call was on Mr Brown, the grocer. When the bell had done its jangling, a tray of candied peel was offered for

inspection. Opinion was divided here, for Jan and I loved the pieces of sugar which had settled within its hollows. Mother considered this wasteful and firmly indicated pieces less attractive. Currants were scooped from a large sack into purple bags before being weighed on Mr Brown's gleaming brass scales.

Those currants were filthy. After washing them thoroughly Mother spread them on a tin tray. We were expected to pick out all the pieces of stalk and leaf, an unrewarding occupation performed only under threat. 'No mince pies, then.' But once the mincemeat was safely sealed in 7 lb stone jars, and the puddings boiled in the copper after washing day, we were at liberty to get on with our own preparations.

These included presents for at least half-a-dozen elderly relatives, and all on the munificence of twopence a week pocket money. The wool bag was ransacked. Surely Aunt Anne would like a holder to hang by the huge iron kettle on the kitchen range. It didn't have to matter if the odd stitches were dropped nor if the last few lines had to be worked in a contrasting colour. Aunt Lizzie could have a sponge cloth mat, for she wouldn't mind the spot of blood in the corner where I pricked my finger.

Before I learnt to knit well enough to make ties, father's present was always a problem until we discovered the fascination of poker work. Wood stolen from his shed lent a certain spice to the project, and the perils of a red-hot poker worked on us as a charm. But we did wish we had learnt to spell the Lord's name for the text 'I am Jehovah' which was to hang above the lawn mower in the tool shed for the next twenty years.

We were not allowed to express any preferences concerning our own presents. I always yearned for one of the stockings which hung in the village shop. Its open net revealed exciting odds and ends such as paper hats in pink tissue, scented

sweets in pallid shades of mauve and orange, and tiny tin pans with fluted edges, ideal for the dolls' stove. The adults considered these 'rubbish' but we were allowed a box of crackers to stow away for the great day. They had usually lost their bang in the damp of Mr Brown's shop.

By mid-December the waits were a nightly visitation. No organised party these, but three or four urchins tunelessly rendering 'Good King Wenceslas' punctuated by much hammering on the door for a coin. Six pennies were piled each night on the chest under the gas lamp in the hall. When that largesse had been distributed nothing further was forthcoming. Bent on self-punishment, we insisted that the singers completed their full repertoire before shuffling on to the next house. It didn't take long.

On 23 December Mother spread out her manger-shaped pie tins and we got busy greasing, filling and snipping, but it often ended in trouble as we stole raw mincemeat or jammed our heavy fingers through the pastry. Once the pies were cooked we set out for Bent Farm at Warburton where Mrs Brown had a plump turkey and several bright sprays of holly waiting for us. The holly was stuck behind the pictures. Along with a Christmas tree which appeared annually from a box in the attic, its emerald green branches sticking out horizontally to receive a few baubles and a piece of tinsel, this was our only decoration. Cards which were delivered on foot by a long-suffering postlady were left on a tray, where we could fingermark them to our hearts' content.

By Christmas Eve the mounting suspense was painful to bear. Piling yew and mistletoe from the garden into a barrow we set off for the church, each taking turns to push. Once there the task of festooning pillars and making the pulpit prickly for the rector had to be done quickly as it was cold, and the difficulty of lighting the oil lamps made it necessary to complete the job before the short winter day closed in. We

stamped our feet and blew on our fingers as we handed up sprays of evergreen, our thoughts directed towards the slices of Christmas cake which would be served in the Parish Room afterwards.

That night we were sent early to bed, for downstairs grown-ups had arrived bearing violins and a 'cello. Those instruments may have been in tune but for us they were sheer torture. How could Father Christmas be expected to come with a noise like that? But come he did. Throughout the early hours we tentatively poked our parcels: at five we were allowed a candle. This was the big moment. All else proved an anti-climax.

Somehow Father Christmas had never guessed quite right. There was a doll when what we really wanted was a pogo-stick and why choose a copy of *The Swiss Family Robinson* which looked exactly like Genesis when *The Tale of Jemima Puddleduck* was so infinitely more attractive? The wooden pencil case with flowers painted on its sliding lid was better, but its single layer did not compare with that belonging to my friend Kay, which had three tiers.

As the turkey went into the oven by the roaring kitchen fire, so we set out for church. In between hymns which we sang lustily, we gazed with apprehension at the decorations, hoping that the frayed string which supported the garlands on the pillars would hold. The final strains of 'Christians Awake', taxing as they were on both choir and congregation, came as an immense relief.

Grandparents came for dinner bringing a box of Turkish Delight, an unfortunate gift as the soft sugar spilt down our velvet dresses and on to the sitting room carpet. However, the gooey stuff compensated for having to keep quiet while the adults slept off their meal. We enjoyed our new *Playbox Annual* even if we did feel a bit sick after a second helping of pudding, accepted in the hope of finding a silver threepenny bit.

After tea, candles were lighted in their sconces and we gathered round the piano. Mother sang a descant to 'The First Nowell' and Grandpa supplied a splendid bass to 'Hark, the Herald Angels'. Soon it was bedtime and for once we did not demur. Wearily rubbing our eyes we staggered upstairs, vaguely aware that tomorrow we must eat up cold turkey and write thank-you letters.

from

The Christmas Book

GYLES BRANDRETH

As the Member of Parliament for Chester, Gyles Brandreth is now on his second (maybe third – or is it fourth?) career. Prior to entering Parliament he was, of course, well known as a radio and television personality and he has written or compiled more than 120 books (at the time of going to press, that is). His mother came from Hoylake and one of his forebears was the famous Victorian journalist and dramatist, George R. Sims, who wrote the never-to-be-forgotten Christmas Day in the Workhouse.

Christmas is special. Christmas is magic. It is a time of warmth and peace. A season when we can revel unashamedly in nostalgia and tradition. The cynics amongst us have described Christmas as a period of preparations, invitations, anticipations, relations, frustrations, prostration and recuperation! But to most of us it is, above all else, a time of celebration. It always has been, and let's hope it always will be.

In the Christian world Christmas is celebrated in remembrance of the birth of Christ. It is literally the 'Mass of Christ'. Yet, strangely, the rituals associated with this religious festival are of pagan origin and were celebrated long before Christ was born.

Since time immemorial it has been man's nature to worship *something*, and because all life seems so dependent on that burning ball of fire in the sky, so vital to the success of harvests, early man went down on his knees and prayed to the sun. In the winter, the strength of the sun being less, it became necessary to slaughter animals for food, and these became the first religious sacrifices. In December, the annual rebirth of the sun turned into an important festival, and many traditions and rituals became established. In Rome on 25 December the *Dies Natalis Invicti Solis* was celebrated – the Birthday of the Unconquered Sun – sacred to Mithras, the god of light, and to Attis, the Phrygian sun god.

The festival was known as the Saturnalia and was a period of celebrations from 17 December right through to the New Year (Kalends) when the Latins rejoiced that the days were getting longer and the power of the sun stronger. It was a time of real merrymaking, when bonfires were lit, homes were decorated with special greenery, people gave each other presents, and there were lots of fun and games. Not blowing up balloons and playing video games, but an early form of charades in which slaves dressed up as their masters, and lords

pretended to be servants, and it is said that people danced through the streets wearing very little but blackened faces and a smile!

These pre-Christian celebrations didn't just take place in Ancient Rome, for at the same time in Europe the winter solstice, when the sun is farthest from the equator and at the point when it appears to be returning, became known as the Festival of Yule. In Britain, France (Gaul), Germany, Denmark, Sweden and especially Norway, the Yule or 'Juul' celebrations became the highlight of the year. Yule logs and candles were lit to the gods Odin and Thor, houses were decorated with evergreens, Yule food and drink were prepared, and mistletoe was ceremoniously cut. Although over two thousand years old, the Yule traditions are still continued today.

In Britain the Druids celebrated the Festival of Nolagh, and it is thought by some that Stonehenge was built as a temple to the sun, constructed in such a way that it cast shadows wherever the sun happened to be. In fact, practically every country in the world, from China to India, from South America to the Middle East, held celebrations at this time of the year. In Greece it was the birthday of Hercules, Ceres and Bacchus (an excuse to indulge in the grape); the Egyptians claimed it as the feast day of Horus; it was not until the fourth century that Pope Julius I decided that 25 December should be celebrated as the birthday of Jesus Christ and Christmas as we know it began.

We now celebrate Christmas every year, but with a little bit of pagan tradition, a Norse Yule log, Druid candles, a drop of wine from Saturnalia, and a feast from the winter solstice. The evergreens and mistletoe still decorate our homes, and each year we continue to give presents to those we love. That's the magic of Christmas.

A Carol for Dolly

ANDREW HAMER

It doesn't lend itself to rendition by a couple of guitars and a recorder, nor can it satisfactorily be sung solo by a thin, reedy, female voice which seems to be the *mode d'emploi* with so many recently-written songs of praise. This one cries out for a bravura contralto or a stentorian baritone or, best of all, a full-throated choir of many voices with a large congregation joining in with gusto. It is that clarion call to Christians everywhere to remember that 25 December is the day on which we celebrate the birthday of Jesus Christ:

> Christians awake! Salute the happy morn
> Whereon the Saviour of the world was born.

Yet it is likely that the first rendition of this famous carol was spoken, not sung, by young Dolly Byrom of Manchester, on Christmas morning 1749, for the writer of those words did not set them to music.

The verses had been written by Dolly's father, Dr John Byrom, celebrated scholar, poet and inventor of a system of shorthand. The inscription read: *Christmas Day for Dolly* and the original manuscript is in the care of Chetham's Library, Manchester.

John Byrom was educated at Chester, then at Merchant Taylors School. In 1708 he entered Trinity College, Cambridge, and achieved a BA degree four years later. In 1714 he was made a Fellow. It was once said of him: 'There

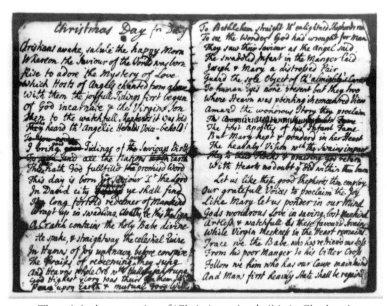

The original manuscript of 'Christians, Awake!' is in Chetham's
Library, Manchester

seems to have been hardly a language of which the literature
was of any value that he did not thoroughly master. Nor was
there any scientific or other literary question agitated by
scholars in his day into which he did not heartily enter.'

He studied medicine but did not practise but needing an
income after his marriage in 1721 to his cousin, Elizabeth
Byrom, he devised a system of shorthand and for twenty-one
years enjoyed a grant from Parliament in return for teaching
it.

And though John Byrom went on to write other verses and
poems which have stood the test of time it is 'Christians
awake!' which remains his best-known work.

But is the carol remembered today for its words or its stirring tune?

For the music to this much-loved hymn we have to thank the one-time organist of Stockport Parish Church, John Wainwright, who was a friend of Byrom's. Byrom recorded in his notebook: 'Christmas Day 1750. The singing men and boys with Mr Wainwright came here and sang "Christians Awake".' That was believed to have been its first performance and later that same day it was repeated in both the Collegiate

The music of this famous carol was written by John Wainwright of Stockport

Church in Manchester (now Manchester Cathedral) and Stockport Parish Church.

Wainwright was born at 58 Churchgate, Stockport, in 1723, the son of a joiner. He grew up to marry a Stockport girl, Ann Clarkson, and they later moved to Manchester where he was among writers and musicians. He was subsequently appointed organist and 'singing man' at the Collegiate Church but it was a post he was to hold for less than a year. He died in January 1768 at the age of only 45 and was buried in the graveyard of Stockport Parish Church. But with the passing of time the exact whereabouts of his grave became lost. According to a local historian he was buried at the west end of the churchyard just inside the gates.

In 1905, John Gordon, a bellringer at the church, stood watching a man build a greenhouse in the Ellis Croft Gardens, Turncroft Lane. He suddenly noticed that one of the pieces of stone being used carried an inscription of some sort. He lifted it up and read:

> Here lieth John Wainwright,
> Organist, Parish Church, Manchester.
> Died 17—

The rector was called to see it and the stone was immediately removed to the churchyard and placed at the foot of the steeple. It was surmised that the gravestone had been one of several damaged by falling masonry when the old church steeple was demolished in 1810.

This discovery served to revive interest in the composer and in 1909 a memorial brass was unveiled in St Mary's Church bearing the inscription:

> In memory of John Wainwright, who was born
> in Stockport, sometime organist of this church,

who left as an heritage to the church at large,
a tune whose sound is gone out into all the lands
where the praise of the Incarnate Lord is sung.
In 1757 he resided at Manchester and became
organist of the Collegiate Church. He was buried
in this Church, January 8th, 1768, aged 45 years.

For many years after his death it was not known that
Wainwright was the composer of this famous tune. In 1767
he published a small volume of music entitled *A Collection of
Psalms, Tunes, Anthems, Hymns and Chants for one, two, three and
four voices* which included 'Christians Awake', but he failed to
put his name to it. In later collections of hymn tunes it was
wrongly attributed to Byrom and later still to one of Byrom's
sons. And with the practice of identifying a hymn tune by its
place of origin it was variously known during the last century
as 'Mottram', 'Leamington', 'Dorchester', 'Huddersfield' and
particularly 'Yorkshire', to name but a few. Today it is known
as 'Stockport'.

Whilst that does not exactly give Wainwright the credit he
deserves the memorial plaque at least puts the record straight.
It provides what antique dealers call 'provenance'. Beneath the
words of tribute are inscribed the opening bars of this much-
sung, much-loved Christmas hymn.

The Donkey's Tale

GLADYS MARY COLES

Gladys Mary Coles lives in West Kirby and is a tutor in Imaginative Writing at both Liverpool universities. But she is best known as an imaginative poet. Seven volumes of her poems have been published and over the years she has won many prizes in national poetry competitions. In 1992 she was selected to represent British poetry in the Euro-Literature Project.

How they found us at all is a mystery –
we didn't know ourselves where we'd be
that night. The Master, he was worried –
slapping me and shouting if I stopped.
It's late! We won't get in anywhere!
He said that over and over. Hard on me, he was –
and I was trying not to rock her or stumble –
her, so patient, patting me. Near her time
poor thing. I know how she felt
(a mother myself, you see).

As I was saying, it's a wonder they found us,
tucked away in a stable. She deserved their gifts –
for the baby, I mean. It was him they came to see.
The shepherds were first, I liked their bleating lamb.
Led by a star they were. And the others –
those from the East, with strange voices.
Rich, riding camels. I was uneasy about them –

The Christmas crib in Chester Cathedral

it was after they left that the trouble started.
Slaughter of new-born boys everywhere.

We had to leave suddenly – at night, hiding
from soldiers. On and on we went,
the Master driving me over rocks and rivers.
We didn't stop except to feed the baby.
By some miracle, we escaped to safety –
a sandy land, miles from home.
It was there that the cross grew in my fur.
One dark line down my back, and another
over my shoulders – just where the baby rested.
I know it was his blessing, this cross.
Seems Jesus blessed me with long life as well –

I'm older than most of my kind. Outlived
my time. Things I've heard lately . . .
A grandson of mine, the other day
carried Jesus into Jerusalem. A triumph it was –
palms spread out in front of his hooves.
Now he's boasting – says the cross in his fur
came directly from the fingers of Jesus.
But I know he inherited it . . .
These young up-and-comings! Wanting everything,
claiming heaven and earth.

The Peace Problem

The Farmer's Reaction to Christmastide

'JOHN BARLEYCORN'

*This pseudonymous view of Christmas, written sixty years ago,
reminds us that for the farmer and his family on a Cheshire
farm it is not a particularly festive season. The farmyard is
full of ghosts and Christmas week is just a week with three
Sundays in it.*

It is very still this Christmas morning. A grey sky; grey haze
everywhere; the countryside so quiet that the slightest sound
carries an incredible distance. Years ago on such a morning as
this you would have heard the boy with the milk float

whistling from a mile away. (Why, I wonder, did the milk lads always whistle as they drove back from the station?) Today there are no milk floats, and the lorries which displaced them came and went with their loads three hours ago. As I stand in the garden I can hear the last beech leaves rustling as they fall; I can hear the red heifer blarting unmusically in my furthermost meadow; and I can hear my neighbour, George Booth, calling down blessings on his stirks. I know what his trouble is. His beasts are out on the road, all his men have gone home, and he's running about in his Sunday trousers trying to round up twelve young cattle by himself. It always happens like that. Why on earth they invariably choose Sundays, Good Fridays and Christmas Days to get out I do not know. But so it is.

Common report has it that pigs are the worst animals to drive. 'There's nothing not so difficult, not to drive, when there's a many on 'em very, isn't a pig.' Personally, I have my doubts. Yearling heifers who have come through a gap on to the road take some beating. Moreover when you've put them back again you've got to find something wherewith to stop up the gap. And as I say, you always have to do it in your Sunday clothes.

I'm sorry for George. He's a good neighbour. But I've been to church and I don't want to change till milking time, so I shall leave him to it. I always reckon to go to church on Christmas morning, even if I don't go any oftener than I might at other times – I'm what the parson calls an outside buttress. I like the first lesson at Mattins – the one about the people that walked in darkness. Old Isaiah must have smacked his lips as he read over the sonorous concatenation that reached its climax in 'the Prince of Peace'. That lesson never sounds so well as in a country church; so strong is the emphasis on peace. And yet somehow there is a hint of sadness about the peace.

The same atmosphere broods over the farmyard. It is very quiet; but it is full of ghosts. We have made a desolation and call it peace. For where are the sleepy-eyed beeves, the fat struggling porkets, the gobling turkeys and those queerly balanced creatures, the runner ducks, with thin, light, graceful heads, and super-stable bases? You, gentle reader, may be able to say where some of them are. All I can tell you is they are gone from here; and they have left behind them their shades. Shades to remind us of bygone labours in rearing and tending, feeding and marketing. I always liked the strawberry roan beast. I remember his mother well. As a calf, a yearling at grass, a feeder in the yard, he always stood out – in a different class altogether from the rest of the bunch. And I wish you could have seen Nancy shutting up the ducks in the dusk of summer evenings – you'd never forget that sight.

There is another side to most pictures, you know; an obverse side to every coin; a subjective as well as an objective view of most questions. As a youngster I was taught that the early bird gets the worm; Mrs Thrush, I was told, always pointed this out to her brood and left them to draw their own conclusion. I was greatly fired by their response until it occurred to me that Mrs Worm couldn't possibly draw the same conclusion from the same facts. Somehow the parable of the prodigal has never appealed to me – it seems so rough on the calf. So it is not surprising that I find an atmosphere of sadness as well as peace in the farmyard.

All the men are, of course, at their homes. They were here for milking this morning and they'll turn up again towards half past three this afternoon. The scientists tell us this early milking in an afternoon is bad for the cows. I believe it is; but what can you do? Folks don't want to be about on the bank at six o'clock on Christmas night. We shall just have to milk early and trust to luck nobody will take a sample tomorrow morning after the long night interval. Or else we shall have to

do it all ourselves; and I'm getting too old to enjoy milking fourteen or fifteen cows at a meal. Christmas Day is very much like a Sunday; except that we generally do a bit of ferreting. Tomorrow will be much the same. Christmas week on the farm is just a week with three Sundays in it; theoretically the other days are full work days, but I notice we never seem to do anything of much account, unless we have to bring up the outlying stock. So generally things are pretty quiet and peaceful.

There is peace of a different sort, though again not without a trace of sadness, within the house. Cheesemaking has, of course, finished – I sold the milk for the winter. The baking is partly finished, too. I suppose the mistress knows how many mince pies we shall eat next week; to me there seems enough food to feed an army, but I don't blame her for making them last week whilse she had the maid. Abigail has gone for a week's holiday, or she has left altogether – I forget which. Maids always change at this time of the year (latterly at every other time of the year as well). So do the farm lads, though as we haven't got any living in now, this doesn't affect us much. There are no 'old fashioned' Christmases in the farm houses now; most of those rollicking foregatherings with old Wardle at Dingley Dell. (To be quite candid I doubt if there ever were. Dickens knew very little about the country, and Micawber is no less a caricature than old Wardle.) It will be with a restrained sort of joy that the family sit down to the Christmas Dinner presently. We have as much good cheer as other folk. But we know that for the next week we've got to do the housework amongst us, and speaking for myself I *do* loathe washing up.

Christmas Greetings

(from a Fairy to a Child)

LEWIS CARROLL

*Cheshire-born 'Lewis Carroll' (Charles Lutwidge Dodgson)
was a mathematics don at Christ Church, Oxford, from
1854 to 1881 and the author of several highly acclaimed
mathematical books. Of a shy and retiring nature he
delighted in the company of children and his two enduring
'Alice' books were first told to Alice Liddell and her two
sisters, the daughters of H.G. Liddell, Dean of Christ
Church, while out on picnics. Alice begged him to write the
story down, he did so and the manuscript with his own
illustrations was given to Alice as a Christmas present in
1865. It was entitled* Alice's Adventures Under Ground.
Re-named Alice's Adventures in Wonderland *it was
published in 1865 with illustrations by Sir John Tenniel and
the original 18,000 words were expanded to 35,000. Two
years later, with Alice's permission, a facsimile of the original
manuscript was published to which Carroll had added an
Introduction and two poems of greetings, one for Easter and
this one for Christmas. All profits from this edition went to
children's hospitals.*

Lady dear, if Fairies may
For a moment lay aside
Cunning tricks and elfish play,
'Tis at happy Christmas-tide.

Lewis Carroll gave the original
manuscript of *Alice's
Adventures Under Ground* to
Alice as a Christmas gift in
1865. This is how he
inscribed it

We have heard the children say –
Gentle children, whom we love –
Long ago, on Christmas Day,
Came a message from above.

Still, as Christmas-tide comes round,
They remember it again –
Echo still the joyful sound
'Peace on earth, good-will to men!'

Yet the hearts must child-like be
Where such heavenly guests abide;
Unto children, in their glee,
All the year is Christmas-tide.

Thus, forgetting tricks and play
For a moment, Lady dear,
We would wish you, if we may,
Merry Christmas, glad New Year!

Christmas, 1867

Corporation Banquets

ANON

The old Corporation of the 'Golden City' of Chester seems to have been at all times renowned for the sumptuousness of their festive meetings; but those given by Earl Grosvenor when he was Mayor have never been surpassed.

It was formerly the custom for the new Chief Magistrate to celebrate the occasion of his being raised to the Civic Chair, by inviting his brethren and friends to dine with him at the commencement of his year of office, and again, in like manner, upon New Year's Day.

On 5 November 1807 the first banquet was given when a temporary floor was erected in the Town Hall so as to be upon a level with the Assembly Room, and the doors of each were taken off. The table in the Town Hall was laid in the form of a horse-shoe, with a table down the centre: on the middle of

which, considerably elevated, stood a noble Baron of Beef, weighing 4 cwt, surmounted by the banner of England and, round the edge of the dish, the words:

'O! the Roast Beef of Old England,
O! the Old English Roast Beef!
Nov. 5, 1807. God Save the King!'

On the same table was also a fine Baron of Mutton, weighing 81 lb, surmounted with his Lordship's Arms neatly painted; and round the edge of this dish his Lordship's motto: 'Nobilitas virtus non stemma character,' – likewise a large ornamental salad, decorated with the city arms and motto: 'Prosperity to the Trade of Chester'.

On the occasion to which we now more expressly allude, the Baron of Mutton was displaced by a large Christmas Pie, decorated in paste with his Lordship's, her Ladyship's, and the city arms; and containing three geese, three turkies, seven hares, twelve partridges, a ham, and a leg of veal, and the whole when baked weighed 154 lb.

The remainder of the Bill of Fare consisted of 4 dishes of codfish and sparlings, 4 dishes of gurnet and sparlings, 6 dishes of stewed carp, 20 tureens of turtle, 4 saddles of mutton, 12 French pies, 4 dishes of bombarded veal, 6 dishes of roasted chickens, 1 round of beef, 4 hams, 3 boiled turkeys and oyster sauce, 12 plum puddings, 6 dishes of maranalled pork, 5 dishes of ducks, 4 loins of marande mutton, 4 dishes of boiled chickens, 4 neats tongues, 6 dishes of oyster patties, 6 legs of mutton, 4 dishes of guinea fowl, 20 hares, 20 necks of venison, 4 dishes of mutton kibob'd, 2 dishes of teal, 10 venison pasties, 3 dishes of wild ducks, 4 dishes of sweet-breads, 4 dishes of à la mode beef, 4 dishes of collared mutton, 12 lemon puddings, 4 dishes of pigeon compote, 6 dishes of veal olives, 8 pigs, 2 dishes of palates and kidneys, 6 geese, 8

dishes of rabbit, 6 pigeon pies, 14 dishes of partridges, 4 dishes of haricot mutton, 17 dishes of Irish pancakes, 20 haunches of venison, 6 dishes of pheasants, 10 dishes of woodcocks.

SWEETS

40 salvers of whips and jellies, 30 moulds of jelly, 20 moulds of blanc-mange, 20 moulds of Dutch flummery, 30 tarts, 48 cheesecakes, 12 dishes of snowballs, 144 puffs.

DESSERT

30 pine apples, 400 dishes of fruit, consisting of peaches, nectarines, grapes, apples, pears, filberts, &c.

The number of guests that sat down on 1 January 1808 was about 200, and on the first occasion about 300, when a similar Bill of Fare was provided.

The rooms were most tastefully fitted up for these princely banquets; and, besides a number of chandeliers, they were illuminated with 3,000 variegated lamps; and on the centre window in the Assembly Room fronting his Lordship's seat were displayed the letters 'G.R.' in variegated lamps.

from

Treasure on Earth

PHYLLIS ELINOR SANDEMAN

The Hon. Mrs Phyllis Elinor Sandeman was the second daughter of the 2nd Lord Newton and her gentle Gaskell-like book is a delightful account of how the festive season was spent at Lyme Park when she was a young girl in the year 1906. As Mrs Gaskell chose to cloak the identity of Knutsford in the anonymity of 'Cranford' so Mrs Sandeman chose to conceal the identities of some of her family and even Lyme Park itself which she called 'Vyne Park'. Lord Legh of Lyme became 'Vayne of Vyne' and she 'demoted' her own father from noble lord to a mere knight, referring to him as 'Sir Thomas Vayne'.
The book was first published in November 1952 and was almost immediately reprinted. When it was re-issued in 1971 (reprinted 1972) a key to the real identities was given.

At this moment the door at the far end of the gallery started to creak open, and gradually from the darkness into the rays of the footlights a group of men appeared bearing a large fir tree. Slowly and carefully they advanced accompanied by a tall commanding figure which took no share of the burden but directed them at every step. At its orders they placed the tree about halfway down the room and some way in front of the stage.

'That will do, thank you.'

Truelove, for it was he, dismissed the gardeners and turned to Phyllis who had left the stage to inspect the tree.

It would have been hard to find a more perfect butler than Truelove (though he preferred to be called 'steward'). He was tall, but not quite so tall as his footmen, and that was as it should be. Immaculate in appearance, rigidly upright, quiet, dignified, confident, there was one thing about him both unconventional and surprising in a butler: his upper lip was closely shaved, but his lower jaw was covered by a grey growth, perfectly kept and trimmed and not unlike King Edward's but still a beard.

There was a rumour that Truelove had a delicate throat which must be protected, but the more probable explanation was that it placed him above the general level, gave him a particular cachet. What Mr Brown of Bayswater could not tolerate on his butler, Sir Thomas Vayne of Vyne could and did. So Truelove had a beard.

'A nice tree, don't you think, miss?' he now remarked to Phyllis.

'Oh, yes, but it's not quite such a good shape as last year's.'

'Ah, wait till I've tied on a few extra branches. Jim, come over here, please, I want you.'

And taking the hint, Phyllis left to get ready for tea.

Truelove was always at his best at Christmas. It gave him a chance to go all out and display to the full his powers of organization. It was as if he said: 'We'll show them what Vyne can do!' Or perhaps more truly: 'What I can do with Vyne'. The tree was his responsibility and no one else was allowed to decorate it. When the children of the estate employees came up on Boxing Day to have tea and receive their presents it was he who acted as master of ceremonies. After tea in the servants' hall, lit for the occasion with Chinese lanterns, they would troop upstairs to the Long Gallery, where the tree in all its glory for the second day in succession provided, except for

The Christmas tree at Lyme Park before the First World War, decorated as always by the butler, Truelove

the blazing fire, the only light in the room. Ready and waiting, rather behind Truelove, Jim Bowden and Gregory the plumber would stand with sponges on the ends of long sticks. Then when everyone had walked round the tree and admired it thoroughly, Truelove would read from a list, not the children's names but the parents' names and their respective ages – a nice distinction.

'Jim Bowden's little girl, aged six years' – and a small girl in her best frock and button boots would clatter across the shiny boards to where Lady Vyne stood beside the tree, receive her gift with a bobbed curtsey and clatter back again.

The servants' hall at Lyme decorated and ready for the children's
Christmas tea party

'George Jackson's little boy, aged six years' – the same
ceremony again, till from the youngest to the eldest they had
all had their presents. Then Truelove would make a speech.

It was the same every year – 'I'm sure we're all very grateful
to her Ladyship for providing this beautiful tree and presents.
When I was a boy and Christmas came round I was pleased if
I got a monkey on a stick. But of course times have changed.
Now I want you all to give three hearty cheers,' etc.

There was always a loyal response. Then the gallery would
resound to the blowing of tin trumpets and whistles, the
clocking of pistols and popping of crackers and the broad
North Country accents of excited young voices.

Arrival at Gawsworth

MRS BRANDT

*The Reverend Francis Brandt MA was curate of Gawsworth
from 1818 to 1844. He and his wife arrived there during the
rectorship of the Reverend Henry Forster Mill who never once
set foot in the parish. In this respect he was no better or worse
than his predecessor or successor, both of whom were
non-resident.
In fact Gawsworth was without a resident rector for almost a
century. The clergy, although receiving rich tithes, were content
to leave things entirely in the hands of poorly paid curates.
This description of the Brandts' arrival at the beautiful
fifteenth-century rectory as newly-weds was told to Thomas
Hughes (1826–90), a distinguished Cheshire antiquary and
historian.*

It was Christmas Eve in the year 1818 that, leaving the high
road, and driving through pretty rural lanes, we entered the
parish of Gawsworth, and first came into sight of the
beautiful old church, destined to be the scene of my husband's
early ministry for five and twenty years!

The day was cold, the trees and hedges leafless and bare;
but they were thickly covered, and the ground was crisped
with a sharp hoar frost. Never shall I forget my first feelings
on looking upon that peaceful, lovely spot! We drove up the

'What a picture did that old rectory house present!' Gawsworth
Rectory dates from the late fifteenth century

green to the little garden gate. What a picture did that old
Rectory House present! It was very old, built of wood and
plaster, gable ended, and painted black and white. Over the
centre porch, projected far out, was a bedroom, which in after
years was named 'Theophila's Bower' after a young friend
who had often slept there. The windows were many shaped
and sized, and glazed with small panes, leaded. This, then,
was to be our home, 'for weal and for woe' – very lovely to
look upon! I thought it so, at any rate; and nothing, to my
memory, can be like it again, as it struck me on the afternoon
of that December day.

Our two maidens came down the garden to meet us (our
man was with us), and quickly following came my husband's
brother, Henry, who had been actively busy to get the
workmen out of the way, and have all things in order for our

reception. This he had done, and soon left us to join his mother and sisters for their Christmas Dinner. It was a strange moment to me – no words can tell it, no pen can paint it!

The porch was entered by a half-glass outer door; within were benches on either side, and inserted in the wall was an iron safe for the registers, with a moulding round of oak, curiously carved. The inner door was like that in our old churches, of heavy oak, studded thickly with large nails and strong and dressed oaken bolts. From this door we passed into a hall, open to the roof – an old-fashioned staircase leading out of it to the best, or state, bedchamber, and to that only. A handsome massive arch was thrown across the middle, and the window was large and filled with coats of arms and other devices in painted glass; it was a beautiful and imposing room to enter! Beyond was a smaller, but good-sized sitting room, with painted cross-beams in the ceiling, held together in the centre by a gilt rose – denoting the silence to be observed respecting all which passed 'beneath the rose' within those walls. The rest of the house was curiously connected, by mysterious little flights of shut-up stairs and winding passages – a dreamy romantic house for two newly-married young people to come to!

We sat down to our first meal soon after, and had scarcely done so when the five silvery bells of our Church rang out a merry peal of welcome to their new Pastor!

Christmas morning came, and our people gathered in the Church. The service was beautifully gone through, as it ever, ever was by him! No, the like will never be heard by me again – I know it, I feel it daily!

The choir consisted of men, with every description of musical instrument under the sun, and when the 10th Anthem was given out to be sung, I rose with the rest of the congregation; and I was feeling very quietly happy, and disposed to be pleased with everything, I have no doubt I

Gawsworth in winter

looked so; until the leader, a man with one eye, laying aside his clarionet, and taking up the solo part, in a cracked voice sang 'Thy wife shall be as the fruitful Vine, &c'. I can feel now the hot flush and tingling sensation which rushed into my cheeks; but everybody looked so serious, and as if it were quite the right and proper form to go through, that I tried to do the same, and stood it out – I believe, however, I ought to have sat still! Then let me record what in after years befel this same anthem. My husband found that it prevented the young married people from coming to church – he therefore ordered that it should not be sung unless by special desire. On the strength of that promise from the Pastor, a young couple made

their first appearance in church; in due time, however, the 10th Anthem appeared on the board. My husband said quietly to the Clerk, 'That must not be sung!' upon which the old man very audibly said 'Yo're desired NOT to sing that anthem!' – still no sign of yielding – there was even a little tuning-up – when the old man, tried past his patience, struck his fist on the desk, and then shaking it at the choir, in a stentorian voice called out 'Yo MUNNA sing that anthem!'. This was decisive – they all sat down, simultaneously abashed; the 'Hundredth Psalm' was put up, and sung, and from that time forward, the 10th Anthem was heard no more in Gawsworth Church!

from

The Vanishing Roads and Other Essays

A Christmas Meditation

RICHARD LE GALLIENNE

Richard Le Gallienne, author of more than fifty books and a close friend of Oscar Wilde, W.B. Yeats and Ernest Rhys, is now largely forgotten, but in the 1890s and early years of this century he was one of the lions of the London and New York literary scenes. He was not only a talented and successful writer, poet and

*essayist but was extremely good-looking. And with his hair
much longer than was fashionable at the time a contemporary
publisher was moved to comment: 'He looks more like a poet
than any man has ever looked before or since'.
His family resided at several different addresses in Birkenhead
as his father moved to more commodious houses on his way up
the management ladder (eventually becoming company secretary)
of the Birkenhead Brewery Company.
What follows is a much abridged version of a lengthy and, by
today's standards, rather circumlocutory essay which he wrote
in 1915.*

Christmas already! However welcome its coming, Christmas
always seems to take us by surprise. Is the year really so soon
at the end of its journey? Why, it seems only yesterday that
it needed a special effort of remembrance to date our letters
with the new *anno domini*. And have you noticed that one
always does that reluctantly, with something almost of
misgiving? The figures of the old year have a warm human
look, but those of the new year wear a chill, unfamiliar,
almost menacing expression. Nineteen hundred and – we
know. It is nearly 'all in'. It has done its best – and its worst.
Between Christmas Day and New Year it has hardly time to
change its character. Good or bad, as it may have been, we
feel at home with it, and we are fain to keep the old almanac
a little longer on the wall. But the last leaves are falling, the
days are shortening. There is a smell of coming snow in the
air, and for weeks past it has already been Christmas in the
shops.

Yes, however it strikes us, we are a year older. On the first of
January last we had twelve brand-new months of a brand-new
year to spend, and now the last of them is all but spent . . .

Strange, that feeling at the end of the year, that somehow
we have missed it, have failed to experience it all to the full,

taken it too carelessly, not dwelt sufficiently on its rich, expressive hours. Each year we feel the same, and however intent we may have been, however we have watched and listened, sensitively eager to hold and exhaust each passing moment, when the year-end has come, we seem somehow to have been cheated after all. Who, at the beginning of each year, has not promised himself a stricter attentiveness to his experience? This year he will 'load every rift with ore'.

Yet, for all our watchfulness, the year seems to have escaped us. We know that the birds sang, the flowers bloomed, that the grass was green, but it seems to us that we did not take our joy of them with sufficient keenness; our sweetheart came, but we did not look deep enough into her eyes. If only we live to see the wild rose again! But meanwhile here is the snow.

Unless we are still numbered among those happy people for whom Christmas trees are laden and lit, this annual prematurity of Christmas cannot but make us a little meditative amid our mirth, and if, while Santa Claus is dispersing his glittering treasures, our thoughts grow a little wistful, they will not necessarily be mournful thoughts, or on that account less seasonable in character; for Christmas is essentially a retrospective feast, and we may, with fitness, with indeed a proper piety of unforgetfulness, bring even our sad memories, as it were to cheer themselves, within the glow of its festivity. Ghosts have always been invited to Christmas parties, and whether they are seen or not, they always come; nor is any form of story so popular by the Christmas fire as the ghost story — which, when one thinks of it, is rather odd, considering the mirthful character of the time. Yet, after all, what are our memories but ghost stories? Ah! the beautiful ghosts that come to the Christmas fire!

Christmas too is pre-eminently the Feast of the Absent, the Festival of the Far-Away, for the most prosperous ingathering of beloved faces about the Christmas fire can but include a

small number of those we would fain have there; and have you ever realized that the absent are ghosts? That is, they live with us sheerly as spiritual presences, dependent upon our faithful remembrance for their embodiment. We may not, with our physical eyes, see them once a year; we may not even have so seen them for twenty years; it may be decreed that we shall never see them again; we seldom, perhaps never, write to each other; all we know of each other is that we are alive and love each other across space and time. Alive – but how? Scarce otherwise, surely, than the unforgotten dead are alive – alive in unforgetting love.

It is rather strange, if you will give it a thought, how much of our real life is thus literally a ghost-story . . . Seldom at Christmas can a mother gather all her children beneath the wing of her smile. Her big boys are seven seas away, and even her girls have Christmas trees of their own. But motherhood is in its very nature a ghostly, a spiritual, thing, and the big boys and the old mother are not really divided. They meet unseen by the Christmas fire, as they meet all the year round in that mysterious ether of the soul, where space and time are not.

Yes, it is strange to think how small a proportion of our lives we spend with those we love; even when we say we spend all our time with them. Husband and wife even – how much of the nearness of the closest of human relations is, and must be, what Rosetti has called 'parted presence'! The man must go forth to his labour until the evening. How few of the twenty-four hours can these two beings who have given their whole lives to each other really give! Husband and wife even must be content to be ghosts to each other for the greater part each day . . .

When I said that the absent were ghosts, I don't think you quite liked the saying. It gave you a little shiver. It seemed rather grimly fantastic. But do you not begin to see what I

mean? Begin to see the comfort of the thought? Begin to see the inner connection between Christmas and the ghost story?

I have a friend who is dead – but I say to myself that he is in New Zealand; for if he were really in New Zealand, we should hardly seem less distant, or be in more frequent communication. We should say that we were both busy men, that the mails were infrequent, but that between us there was no need of words, that we both 'understood'. That is what I say now. It is just as appropriate. Perhaps he says it too. And – we shall meet by the Christmas fire.

I have a friend who is alive. He is alive in England. We have not met for twelve years. He never writes, and I never write. Perhaps we shall never meet, never even write to each other, again. It is our way, the way of many a friendship, none the less real for its silence – friendship by faith, one might say, rather than by correspondence. My dead friend is not more dumb, not more invisible. When these two friends meet me by the Christmas fire, will they not both alike be ghosts – both, in a sense, dead, but, both, in a truer sense, alive?

And, when you think of it, is not this festival founded upon what, without irreverence, we may call the Divine Ghost Story of Christmas? Was there ever another ghost story so strange, so full of marvels, a story with so thrilling a message from the unseen? Taken just as a story, is there anything in the *Arabian Nights* so marvellous as this ghost story of Christmas?

The world was all marble and blood and bronze, against a pitiless sky of pitiless gods. The world was Rome. . .

And against all this marble and blood and bronze, what frail fantastic attack is this? What quaint expedition from fairyland that comes so insignificantly against these battlements on which the Roman helmets catch the setting sun?

A Star in the Sky. Some Shepherds from Judea. Three Wise Men from the East. Some Frankincense and Myrrh. A Mother and Child.

Yes, a fairytale procession – but these are to conquer Rome, and that child at his mother's breast has but to speak three words, for all that marble and bronze to melt away: 'Love One Another'.

It may well have seemed an almost ludicrous weapon – three gentle words. So one might attack a fortress with a flower. But Rome fell before them, for all that, and cruel as the world is, so cruel a world can never be again. The history of Christianity . . . is the history of a ghost story.

Christmas is the friendly human announcement of this ghostly truth; its holly and boar's head are but a rough-and-tumble emblazonment of that mystic gospel of – The Three Words; the Gospel of the Unseen Love.

But enough of ghostly, grown-up thoughts. Let us end with a song for the children:

> O the big red sun,
> And the wide white world,
> And the nursery window
> Mother-of-pearled;
>
> And the houses all
> In hoods of snow,
> And the mince-pies,
> And the mistletoe;
>
> And the Christmas pudding,
> And berries red,
> And stockings hung
> At the foot of the bed;
>
> And carol-singers,
> And nothing but play –
> O baby, this is
> Christmas Day!

THE ancient halls of England! the palace of our Queen,
   The mansions of our noblemen! the cottage on the green
A merry, merry Christmas, I wish to one and all;
Also a happy opening year, with health to crown the whole.

In all the towns of England, both old and young may hear
The bands of Christmas music, which come but once a year,
Your Postman—he comes daily, in all the seasons round,
He brings you all the best news that in the world is found.

He brings you news from foreign lands—from sons and daughters
From relatives on every hand, more than once a year,   [dear.
He now entreats with confidence, while waiting at your door,
Your usual Christmas recompense, as liberal as before.

   The Postman of this district begs most respectfully to present
to you the Compliments of the Season, and hopes that the important duties which have devolved upon him have been so dis-
charged as to be favourably remembered at this joyous and festive
Season.   Yours respectfully,

JOSEPH TIMPSON.

A broad hint from a very enterprising postman in Victorian times

Festive Initiation

GLADYS MARY COLES

Behind glass, in the corner cupboard,
circles of gold, rose-rimmed,
large and small moons.
Unlocking her wedding-ware
for the once-yearly ceremony of use,
she carried each one like a fragile child
to its ritual place on the elongated table.
This bone-thin reverence, part of Christmas –
chill plates I feared to touch, or taste
their pale offering of poultry flakes,
or fork the stubborn marble-pickles.

Within the parlour's gloom, a coffin-shape –
the rosewood pianola,
his paid-for pride's possession.
He took me in to listen, opened the long lid,
laid in Rachmaninov in a perforated roll.
Adjusting coat and sleeves, he pumped the pedals,
mock finger-movements making music.
At last, my turn: he let me try with Liszt –
I barely reached the pedals, stretching, pushing
to release Beethoven, press on through Bach.
In imaginary concert halls I triumphed
with Mozart, Schumann, Chopin – until,
legs locked, I was half-carried home.

Sometimes now, when cycling up steep gradients,
I pedal to Ravel, the relentless *Bolero*,
and think of Grandad, his rosewood coffin-music-box;
or glimpsing wild roses in the hedges,
I remember Grandma, her cold cabinet of gold.

Christmas Storms
and Sunshine

ELIZABETH GASKELL

Mrs Gaskell shares pride of place with Lewis Carroll
as Cheshire's best-known writer. Her father was a Unitarian
minister in London but after the death
of her mother when Elizabeth was only a year old
Aunt Hannah Lumb agreed to look after her and
brought her back to Knutsford.
Knutsford, of course, later served as a role model for her famous
classic novel of small-town life Cranford *and as Hollingford in*
Wives and Daughters *which was published after her death.*
This short story, Christmas Storms and Sunshine, *was a*
fairly early literary attempt by Mrs Gaskell and for some
reason she chose to use the curious pen-name of 'Cotton Mather
Mills'. It was first published in 1848 in Howitts' Journal, *a*

*literary weekly launched by her friends, William and Mary
Howitt of Manchester. Alas, the magazine, which was intended
to raise the cultural level of the working classes, failed
completely in its noble objectives and led to the Howitts'
bankruptcy two years later.
Elizabeth Gaskell died in 1865 and is buried in the graveyard
of Knutsford's Unitarian Chapel.*

In the town of – (no matter where) there circulated two local newspapers (no matter when). Now the *Flying Post* was long-established and respectable – alias bigoted and Tory; the *Examiner* was spirited and intelligent – alias newfangled and democratic. Every week these newspapers contained articles abusing each other, as cross and peppery as articles could be, and evidently the production of irritated minds, although they seemed to have one stereotyped commencement – 'Though the article appearing in our last week's *Post* (or *Examiner)* is below contempt, yet we have been induced,' &c. &c.; and every Saturday the Radical shopkeepers shook hands together, and agreed that the *Post* was done for by the slashing, clever *Examiner*; while the more dignified Tories began by regretting that Johnson should think that low paper, only read by a few of the vulgar, worth wasting his wit upon; however, the *Examiner* was at its last gasp.

It was not, though. It lived and flourished; at least it paid its way, as one of the heroes of my story could tell. He was chief compositor, or whatever title may be given to the headman of the mechanical part of a newspaper. He hardly confined himself to that department. Once or twice, unknown to the editor, when the manuscript had fallen short, he had filled up the vacant space by compositions of his own; announcements of a forthcoming crop of green peas in December; a grey thrush having been seen, or a white hare, or such interesting phenomena; invented for the occasion, I must confess; but what

of that? His wife always knew when to expect a little specimen of her husband's literary talent by a peculiar cough, which served as prelude; and, judging from this encouraging sign, and the high-pitched and emphatic voice in which he read them, she was inclined to think that an 'Ode to an early Rosebud,' in the corner devoted to original poetry, and a letter in the correspondence department, signed 'Pro Bono Publico,' were her husband's writing, and to hold up her head accordingly.

I never could find out what it was that occasioned the Hodgsons to lodge in the same house as the Jenkinses. Jenkins held the same office in the Tory Paper as Hodgson did in the *Examiner*, and, as I said before, I leave you to give it a name. But Jenkins had a proper sense of his position, and a proper reverence for all in authority, from the king down to the editor and sub-editor. He would as soon have thought of borrowing the king's crown for a nightcap, or the king's sceptre for a walking-stick as he would have thought of filling up any spare corner with any production of his own; and I think it would have even added to his contempt of Hodgson (if that were possible), had he known of the 'productions of his brain,' as the latter fondly alluded to the paragraphs he inserted, when speaking to his wife.

Jenkins had his wife too. Wives were wanting to finish the completeness of the quarrel which existed one memorable Christmas week, some dozen years ago, between the two neighbours, the two compositors. And with wives, it was a very pretty, a very complete quarrel. To make the opposing parties still more equal, still more well-matched, if the Hodgsons had a baby ('such a baby! – a poor, puny little thing'), Mrs Jenkins had a cat ('such a cat! a great, nasty, miowling tom-cat, that was always stealing the milk put by for little Angel's supper'). And now, having matched Greek with Greek, I must proceed to the tug of war. It was the day before Christmas; such a cold east wind! such an inky sky! such a blue-black look in people's faces,

as they were driven out more than usual, to complete their purchases for the next day's festival.

Before leaving home that morning, Jenkins had given some money to his wife to buy the next day's dinner.

'My dear, I wish for turkey and sausages. It may be a weakness, but I own I am partial to sausages. My deceased mother was. Such tastes are hereditary. As to the sweets — whether plum pudding or mince pies — I leave such considerations to you; I only beg you not to mind expense. Christmas comes but once a year.'

And again he called out from the bottom of the first flight of stairs, just close to the Hodgsons' door ('such ostentatiousness,' as Mrs Hodgson observed), 'You will not forget the sausages, my dear!'

'I should have liked to have had something above common, Mary,' said Hodgson, as they too made their plans for the next day; 'but I think roast beef must do for us. You see, love, we've a family.'

'Only one, Jem! I don't want more than roast beef, though, I'm sure. Before I went to service, mother and me would have thought roast beef a very fine dinner.'

'Well, let's settle it, then, roast beef and a plum pudding; and now, goodbye. Mind and take care of little Tom. I thought he was a bit hoarse this morning.'

And off he went to his work.

Now, it was a good while since Mrs Jenkins and Mrs Hodgson had spoken to each other, although they were quite as much in possession of the knowledge of events and opinions as though they did. Mary knew that Mrs Jenkins despised her for not having a real lace cap, which Mrs Jenkins had; and for having been a servant, which Mrs Jenkins had not; and the little occasional pinchings which the Hodgsons were obliged to resort to, to make both ends meet, would have been very patiently endured by Mary, if she had not

winced under Mrs Jenkins's knowledge of such economy. But she had her revenge. She had a child, and Mrs Jenkins had none. To have had a child, even such a puny baby as little Tom, Mrs Jenkins would have worn commonest caps, and cleaned grates, and drudged her fingers to the bone. The great unspoken disappointment of her life soured her temper, and turned her thoughts inward, and made her morbid and selfish.

'Hang that cat! he's been stealing again! he's gnawed the cold mutton in his nasty mouth till it's not fit to set before a Christian; and I've nothing else for Jem's dinner. But I'll give it him now I've caught him, that I will!'

So saying, Mary Hodgson caught up her husband's Sunday cane, and despite pussy's cries and scratches, she gave him such a beating as she hoped might cure him of his thievish propensities; when, lo! and behold, Mrs Jenkins stood at the door with a face of bitter wrath.

'Aren't you ashamed of yourself, ma'am, to abuse a poor dumb animal, ma'am, as knows no better than to take food when he sees it, ma'am? He only follows the nature which God has given, ma'am; and it's a pity your nature, ma'am, which I've heard is of the stingy saving species, does not make you shut your cupboard door a little closer. There is such a thing as law for brute animals. I'll ask Mr Jenkins, but I don't think them Radicals has done away with that law yet, for all their Reform Bill, ma'am. My poor precious love of a Tommy, is he hurt? and is his leg broke for taking a mouthful of scraps, as most people would give away to a beggar – if he'd take 'em!' wound up Mrs Jenkins, casting a contemptuous look on the remnant of a scrag end of mutton.

Mary felt very angry and very guilty. For she really pitied the poor limping animal as he crept up to his mistress, and there lay down to bemoan himself; she wished she had not beaten him so hard, for it certainly was her own careless way

of never shutting the cupboard door that had tempted him to his fault. But the sneer at her little bit of mutton turned her penitence to fresh wrath, and she shut the door in Mrs Jenkins's face, as she stood caressing her cat in the lobby, with such a bang, that it wakened little Tom, and he began to cry.

Everything was to go wrong with Mary today. Now baby was awake, who was to take her husband's dinner to the office? She took the child in her arms and tried to hush him off to sleep again, and as she sung she cried, she could hardly tell why – a sort of reaction from her violent angry feelings. She wished she had never beaten the poor cat; she wondered if his leg was really broken. What would her mother say if she knew how cross and cruel her little Mary was getting? If she should live to beat her child in one of her angry fits?

It was of no use lullabying while she sobbed so; it must be given up, and she must just carry her baby in her arms, and take him with her to the office, for it was long past dinnertime. So she pared the mutton carefully, although by so doing she reduced the meat to an infinitesimal quantity, and taking the baked potatoes out of the oven, she popped them piping hot into her basket, with the et-cæteras of plate, butter, salt, and knife and fork.

It was, indeed, a bitter wind. She bent against it as she ran, and the flakes of snow were sharp and cutting as ice. Baby cried all the way, though she cuddled him up in her shawl. Then her husband had made his appetite up for a potato pie, and (literary man as he was) his body got so much the better of his mind, that he looked rather black at the cold mutton. Mary had no appetite for her own dinner when she arrived at home again. So, after she had tried to feed baby, and he had fretfully refused to take his bread and milk, she laid him down as usual on his quilt, surrounded by playthings, while she sided away, and chopped suet for the next day's pudding.

Early in the afternoon a parcel came, done up first in brown paper, then in such a white, grass-bleached, sweet-smelling towel, and a note from her dear, dear mother; in which quaint writing she endeavoured to tell her daughter that she was not forgotten at Christmas time; but that, learning that Farmer Burton was killing his pig, she had made interest for some of his famous pork, out of which she had manufactured some sausages, and flavoured them just as Mary used to like when she lived at home.

'Dear, dear mother!' said Mary to herself. 'There never was any one like her for remembering other folk. What rare sausages she used to make! Home things have a smack with 'em no bought things can ever have. Set them up with their sausages! I've a notion if Mrs Jenkins had ever tasted mother's she'd have no fancy for them townmade things Fanny took in just now.'

And so she went on thinking about home, till the smiles and the dimples came out again at the remembrance of that pretty cottage, which would look green even now in the depth of winter, with its pyracanthus, and its holly-bushes, and the great Portugal laurel that was her mother's pride. And the back path through the orchard to Farmer Burton's, how well she remembered it! The bushels of unripe apples she had picked up there and distributed among his pigs, till he had scolded her for giving them so much green trash!

She was interrupted – her baby (I call him a baby, because his father and mother did, and because he was so little of his age, but I rather think he was eighteen months old,) had fallen asleep some time before among his playthings; an uneasy, restless sleep; but of which Mary had been thankful, as his morning's nap had been too short, and as she was so busy. But now he began to make such a strange crowing noise, just like a chair drawn heavily and gratingly along a kitchen floor! His eyes were open, but expressive of nothing but pain.

'Mother's darling!' said Mary, in terror, lifting him up. 'Baby, try not to make that noise. Hush, hush, darling; what hurts him?' But the noise came worse and worse.

'Fanny! Fanny!' Mary called in mortal fright, for her baby was almost black with his gasping breath, and she had no one to ask for aid or sympathy but her landlady's daughter, a little girl of twelve or thirteen, who attended to the house in her mother's absence, as daily cook in gentlemen's families. Fanny was more especially considered the attendant of the upstairs lodgers (who paid for the use of the kitchen, 'for Jenkins could not abide the smell of meat cooking'), but just now she was fortunately sitting at her afternoon's work of

Knutsford Unitarian Chapel where Elizabeth Gaskell was married and lies buried

darning stockings, and hearing Mrs Hodgson's cry of terror, she ran to her sitting room, and understood the case at a glance.

'He's got the croup! O Mrs Hodgson, he'll die as sure as fate. Little brother had it, and he died in no time. The doctor said he could do nothing for him – it had gone too far. He said if we'd put him in a warm bath at first, it might have saved him; but, bless you! he was never half so bad as your baby.' Unconsciously there mingled in her statement some of a child's love of producing an effect; but the increasing danger was clear enough.

'Oh, my baby! my baby! Oh, love, love! don't look so ill! I cannot bear it. And my fire so low! There, I was thinking of home, and picking currants, and never minding the fire. O Fanny! what is the fire like in the kitchen? Speak.'

'Mother told me to screw it up,.and throw some slack on as soon as Mrs Jenkins had done with it, and so I did. It's very low and black. But, oh, Mrs Hodgson! let me run for the doctor – I cannot bear to hear him, it's so like little brother.'

Through her streaming tears Mary motioned her to go; and trembling, sinking, sick at heart, she laid her boy in his cradle, and ran to fill her kettle.

Mrs Jenkins, having cooked her husband's snug little dinner, to which he came home; having told him her story of pussy's beating, at which he was justly and dignifiedly (?) indignant, saying it was all of a piece with that abusive *Examiner*; having received the sausages, and turkey, and mince-pies, which her husband had ordered; and cleaned up the room, and prepared everything for tea, and coaxed and duly bemoaned her cat (who had pretty nearly forgotten his beating, but very much enjoyed the petting); having done all these and many other things, Mrs Jenkins sat down to get up the real lace cap. Every thread was pulled out separately, and carefully stretched: when – what was that?

Outside, in the street, a chorus of piping children's voices
sang the old carol she had heard a hundred times in the days
of her youth:

> 'As Joseph was a walking he heard an angel sing,
> "This night shall be born our heavenly King.
> He neither shall be born in housen nor in hall,
> Nor in the place of Paradise, but in an ox's stall.
> He neither shall be clothed in purple nor in pall,
> But all in fair linen, as were babies all:
> He neither shall be rocked in silver nor in gold,
> But in a wooden cradle that rocks on the mould,"' &c

She got up and went to the window. There, below, stood
the group of black little figures, relieved against the snow,
which now enveloped everything. 'For old sake's sake,' as she
phrased it, she counted out a halfpenny apiece for the singers,
out of the copper bag, and threw them down below.

The room had become chilly while she had been counting out
and throwing down her money, so she stirred her already
glowing fire, and sat down right before it – but not to stretch
her lace; like Mary Hodgson, she began to think over long past
days, on softening remembrances of the dead and gone, on words
long forgotten, on holy stories heard at her mother's knee.

'I cannot think what's come over me tonight,' said she, half
aloud, recovering herself by the sound of her own voice from
her train of thought – 'My head goes wandering on them old
times. I'm sure more texts have come into my head with
thinking on my mother within this last half-hour, than I've
thought on for years and years. I hope I'm not going to die.
Folks says, thinking too much on the dead betokens we're
going to join 'em; I should be loth to go just yet – such a fine
turkey as we've got for dinner tomorrow too!'

Knock, knock, knock, at the door, as fast as knuckles could

go. And then, as if the comer could not wait, the door was opened, and Mary Hodgson stood there as white as death.

'Mrs Jenkins! – oh, your kettle is boiling, thank God! Let me have the water for my baby, for the love of God! He's got croup, and is dying!'

Mrs Jenkins turned on her chair with a wooden, inflexible look on her face, that (between ourselves) her husband knew and dreaded for all his pompous dignity.

'I'm sorry I can't oblige you, ma'am; my kettle is wanted for my husband's tea. Don't be afeared, Tommy, Mrs Hodgson won't venture to intrude herself where she's not desired. You'd better send for the doctor, ma'am, instead of wasting your time in wringing your hands, ma'am – my kettle is engaged.'

Mary clasped her hands together with passionate force, but spoke no word of entreaty to that wooden face – that sharp, determined voice; but, as she turned away, she prayed for strength to bear the coming trial, and strength to forgive Mrs Jenkins.

Mrs Jenkins watched her go away meekly, as one who has no hope, and then she turned upon herself as sharply as she ever did on any one else.

'What a brute I am, Lord forgive me! What's my husband's tea to a baby's life? In croup, too, where time is everything. You crabbed old vixen, you! – any one may know you never had a child!'

She was downstairs (kettle in hand) before she had finished her self-upbraiding; and when in Mrs Hodgson's room, she rejected all thanks (Mary had not the voice for many words), saying, stiffly, 'I do it for the poor babby's sake, ma'am, hoping he may live to have mercy to poor dumb beasts, if he does forget to lock his cupboards'.

But she did everything, and more than Mary, with her young inexperience, could have thought of. She prepared the

warm bath, and tried it with her husband's own thermometer (Mr Jenkins was as punctual as clockwork in noting down the temperature of every day). She let his mother place her baby in the tub, still preserving the same rigid, affronted aspect, and then she went upstairs without a word. Mary longed to ask her to stay, but dared not; though, when she left the room, the tears chased each other down her cheeks faster than ever. Poor young mother! how she counted the minutes till the doctor should come. But, before he came, down again stalked Mrs Jenkins, with something in her hand.

'I've seen many of these croup-fits, which, I take it, you've not, ma'am. Mustard plaisters is very sovereign, put on the throat; I've been up and made one, ma'am, and, by your leave, I'll put it on the poor little fellow.'

Mary could not speak, but she signed her grateful assent.

It began to smart while they still kept silence; and he looked up to his mother as if seeking courage from her looks to bear the stinging pain; but she was softly crying to see him suffer, and her want of courage reacted upon him, and he began to sob aloud. Instantly Mrs Jenkins's apron was up, hiding her face: 'Peep-bo, baby,' said she, as merrily as she could. His little face brightened, and his mother having once got the cue, the two women kept the little fellow amused, until his plaister had taken effect.

'He's better – oh, Mrs Jenkins, look at his eyes! how different! And he breathes quite softly.'

As Mary spoke thus, the doctor entered. He examined his patient. Baby was really better.

'It has been a sharp attack, but the remedies you have applied have been worth all the Pharmacopœia an hour later. I shall send a powder,' &c &c.

Mrs Jenkins stayed to hear this opinion; and (her heart wonderfully more easy) was going to leave the room, when Mary seized her hand and kissed it; she could not speak her gratitude.

Mrs Jenkins looked affronted and awkward, and as if she must go upstairs and wash her hand directly.

But, in spite of these sour looks, she came softly down an hour or so afterwards to see how baby was.

The little gentleman slept well after the fright he had given his friends; and on Christmas morning, when Mary awoke and looked at the sweet little pale face lying on her arm, she could hardly realise the danger he had been in.

When she came down (later than usual), she found the household in a commotion. What do you think had happened? Why, pussy had been traitor to his best friend, and eaten up some of Mr Jenkins's own especial sausages; and gnawed and tumbled the rest so, that they were not fit to be eaten! There were no bounds to that cat's appetite! he would have eaten his own father if he had been tender enough. And now Mrs Jenkins stormed and cried – 'Hang the cat!'

Christmas Day, too! and all the shops shut! 'What was turkey without sausages?' gruffly asked Mr Jenkins.

'O Jem!' whispered Mary, 'hearken what a piece of work he's making about sausages – I should like to take Mrs Jenkins up some of mother's; they're twice as good as bought sausages.'

'I see no objection, my dear. Sausages do not involve intimacies, else his politics are what I can no ways respect.'

'But, oh, Jem, if you had seen her last night about baby! I'm sure she may scold me for ever, and I'll not answer. I'd even make her cat welcome to the sausages.' The tears gathered to Mary's eyes as she kissed her boy.

'Better take 'em upstairs, my dear, and give them to the cat's mistress.' And Jem chuckled at his saying.

Mary put them on a plate, but still she loitered.

'What must I say, Jem? I never know.'

'Say – I hope you'll accept of these sausages, as my mother

— no, that's not grammar; — say what comes uppermost, Mary, it will be sure to be right.'

So Mary carried them upstairs and knocked at the door; and when told to 'come in,' she looked very red, but went up to Mrs Jenkins, saying, 'Please take these. Mother made them.' And was away before an answer could be given.

Just as Hodgson was ready to go to church, Mrs Jenkins came downstairs, and called Fanny. In a minute, the latter entered the Hodgsons' room, and delivered Mr and Mrs Jenkins's compliments, and they would be particular glad if Mr and Mrs Hodgson would eat their dinner with them.

'And carry baby upstairs in a shawl, be sure,' added Mrs Jenkins's voice in the passage, close to the door, whither she had followed her messenger. There was no discussing the matter, with the certainty of every word being overheard.

Mary looked anxiously at her husband. She remembered his saying he did not approve of Mr Jenkins's politics.

'Do you think it would do for baby?' asked he.

'Oh, yes,' answered she eagerly; 'I would wrap him up so warm.'

'And I've got our room up to sixty-five already, for all it's so frosty,' added the voice outside.

Now, how do you think they settled the matter? The very best way in the world. Mr and Mrs Jenkins came down into the Hodgsons' room and dined there. Turkey at the top, roast beef at the bottom, sausages at one side, potatoes at the other. Second course, plum pudding at the top, and mince pies at the bottom.

And after dinner, Mrs Jenkins would have baby on her knee, and he seemed quite to take to her; she declared he was admiring the real lace on her cap, but Mary thought (though she did not say so) that he was pleased by her kind looks and coaxing words. Then he was wrapped up and carried carefully upstairs to tea, in Mrs Jenkins's room. And after tea, Mrs Jenkins, and Mary, and her husband, found out each other's mutual liking for music, and sat singing old glees and

catches, till I don't know what o'clock, without one word of politics or newspapers.

Before they parted, Mary had coaxed pussy on to her knee; for Mrs Jenkins would not part with baby, who was sleeping on her lap.

'When you're busy bring him to me. Do, now, it will be a real favour. I know you must have a deal to do, with another coming; let him come up to me. I'll take the greatest of cares of him; pretty darling, how sweet he looks when he's asleep!'

When the couples were once more alone, the husbands unburdened their minds to their wives.

Mr Jenkins said to his – 'Do you know, Burgess tried to make me believe Hodgson was such a fool as to put paragraphs into the *Examiner* now and then; but I see he knows his place, and has got too much sense to do any such thing.'

Hodgson said – 'Mary, love, I almost fancy from Jenkins's way of speaking (so much civiler than I expected), he guesses I wrote that "Pro Bono" and the "Rosebud" – at any rate, I've no objection to your naming it, if the subject should come uppermost; I should like him to know I'm a literary man.'

Well! I've ended my tale; I hope you don't think it too long; but, before I go, just let me say one thing.

If any of you have any quarrels, or misunderstandings, or coolnesses, or cold shoulders, or shynesses, or tiffs, or miffs, or huffs, with any one else, just make friends before Christmas – you will be so much merrier if you do.

I ask it of you for the sake of that old angelic song, heard so many years ago by the shepherds, keeping watch by night, on Bethlehem Heights.

An Old Cheshire Christmas

CUTHBERT BRIDGEWATER

They say Charles Dickens invented a Christmas that never existed beyond his imagination. This may be true; but the secular festival is ever-changing, and my earliest-remembered Christmas in my mother's old home near Chester, at the turn of the century, was quite different from Christmas in these gadgetry days of television. I think this is because our fun – and we had plenty – was home-made. We entertained ourselves.

The family was large and when, shortly before the holiday, sons, daughters and grandchildren arrived (always in time for the important pudding-boiling on Christmas Eve) it was like an invasion. Beforehand, my normally abstemious grandfather prepared his usual strange concoction, his own brew of 'lambswool'. Compounded of wine, spices, ginger, sugar, and soggy toast-cubes, it looked revolting, though grown-ups seemed to enjoy it, topped off as it was with white Jamaica rum.

While everyone told their news and sipped the drink, my grandfather gathered the children round his chair to hear stories of his boyhood, some of which I still remember. He spoke of Thomassing or the begging from house to house by poor people for corn or what they could get. This took place on St Thomas's Day, 21 December, when Christmas festivities

formerly began. Local millers ground the corn free so that poor people could bake their Christmas cakes and bread. It was stranger to hear the old man, a bearded, patriarchal figure, talking of burning his fingers in snap-dragons, those bowls of raisins floating in blazing liquor, which he called flapdragons. I remember, too, him repeating the lovely legend that, at midnight on Christmas Eve, cows knelt in their shippons because Christ was once laid near them. I wondered how cattle, made as they are, could kneel with their back legs. It was puzzling.

When the gardener brought in the big tree-root, which he called the Yule clog, my grandfather solemnly warned my mother that, while it burned, no barefooted or squinting person should be admitted, or bad luck would result. My lace-clad grandmother, whose early acquaintance with a back-board showed in her unvaryingly erect carriage, nodded gravely and I wondered why strabismic, unshod persons should call on Christmas Eve anyway. I didn't risk mentioning this as I was temporarily under a cloud, having knocked over and spoiled a large bowl of my grandmother's damson-cheese which had been left on the table to cool.

When twelve struck, my sister was asked to let Christmas in. Frightened to death, she stole to the heavy door and after opening it raced back again; though what she expected to see on the step, she never explained. But before this, everyone had fun with the decorations, many of which were of ivy which grandmother said was lucky for women. This was perhaps an odd idea as she had two unmarried daughters out of her seven-strong family. Holly, it seemed, favoured menfolk; but the magical all-heal of mistletoe was good for everyone.

My mother has told me that when she was a girl, instead of mistletoe Cheshire folk often hung up large evergreen

A Christmas market in Elizabeth Gaskell's time

bunches, tied, tinselled and lit by candles. Called kissing-bunches, they included a clump of mistletoe to make their purpose clear.

All decorations were removed before 1 February; if not, the next day, Candlemas, they would turn into goblins. After

Christmas had been invited in, the many stockings, each labelled, were hung up in the large tiled kitchen.

Christmas Day, following the excitement of opening presents, was plethoric; for after church the day was given over (in my case at least) to eating. That afternoon, a mischievous uncle suggested lighting a bonfire to wake us up, while the elders chatted in the drawing room. This seemed a good idea, though our eldest aunt, a frigid spinster of narrow principles, said it would be a sin, and her parting shot: 'What will father say?' made us uneasy. However, after ranging over the eight-acre gardens and orchard for whatever we could find, we raised a blaze and roasted potatoes and chestnuts.

Everything was going splendidly when the old gentleman emerged. We suspected the aunt of telling tales; but her time was coming. She was to crown the holiday with a prize gaffe. The atmosphere was strained until the vicar arrived for afternoon tea. My aunt, who always went girlish at the sight of a clerical collar made the tea from a boiling spirit-kettle, and presently poured out an attenuated liquid that was unmistakable. 'How silly of me,' she twittered, 'I've made water'; a splendid remark which consoled us all for the spoiled bonfire.

Later on we played charades and other games, and after several rounds of consequences we sang carols, 'The Holly and the Ivy' and some ballads. One uncle sang something like 'Had I the wings of a dove, I'd flee,' and a pert young cousin wanted to know what a dove-eyed flea was. Soon it was bedtime and, deeply depressed by my father's remark that Christmas was as far off as ever, we retired. It was some time before I dropped off. An owl hooted in the orchard, turning my thoughts to ghosts. I wondered if, at night, the stone coffin in the ruined walls of St John's was *always* empty – a thought that did not induce sleep.

Customs Quaint
and Curious

*In many parts of the country in less sophisticated times
Christmas and New Year were occasions for indulging in all
manner of odd behaviour. Most of these quaint and curious
customs were of pagan origin but those taking part in the
proceedings would probably not know that — or care much if
they did. But for some reason Cheshire folk made more of All
Souls' Day (1 November) than they did of Christmas.*

On that day Cheshire folk went 'souling' and performed a
traditional Mumming Play which was known as the Soul-
Caking Play. Two exceptions to this, however, were Alderley
and Bromborough in Wirral. There the Mumming Plays were
performed at Christmas and, in the latter place, not a word
was spoken; it was all mimed. But since the plot was fairly
uniform throughout the county everyone understood.

Souling was, like Guy Fawkes night and the carol singing
season, an opportunity for children and young people to
extract money from their elders. Groups of them would go
round the houses in a village or town singing a Souling Song
which brought them rewards of money and/or specially-baked
Souling Cakes.

The Souling Song differed slightly from village to village
but in the version recorded by the great baritone, Owen
Brannigan, the chorus went like this:

> A-soul, a-soul, a-soul cake!
> Please, good missus, a soul cake;

An apple, a pear, a plum or a cherry,
Any good thing to make us all merry;
One for Peter, two for Paul, three for Him
who made us all.

Souling cakes were small, spicy, sweetened buns specially
baked by householders for the occasion. In some villages the
souling party included a youth draped in a white sheet
wearing a horse's head with a mouth which, like the Chinese
New Year dragons, opened and shut. His prancing about and
general antics were known as 'hodening'. In the village of
Over (now part of Winsford) they dispensed with the horse
but the soulers went round with blackened faces.

Mumming plays, wherever they were performed and whatever
season of the year, were, like pantomimes, basically the same.
Cheshire Soul-Caking Plays began with an introduction followed
by a fierce dispute between two characters, one of whom is killed.
A doctor appears on the scene and miraculously restores the man
to life. And that's it, really. Various other characters are included
to flesh it out and, in Cheshire, the horse was introduced.
Different villages had differing versions with characters bearing
different names but the plays were never written down and the
basic plot remained unchanged down the centuries.

Despite this great concentration on All Souls' Day there were
certain traditional practices observed during the Christmas
season. 'Curning' was one of them when the poor people of the
parish (usually the womenfolk) would carry a sack from house
to house into which the householder would pour a pint, or
sometimes a quart, of grain. When the sack was full it was
taken to the local miller who, in good Christian spirit, would
grind it for them free of charge. The word 'curning' is thought
to be a contraction of 'corn-begging' and the practice was
always observed on St Thomas's Day, 21 December.

The donated flour was used for making Christmas cakes

The Chester Village Players performing one of the Chester Mystery
Plays on the village green at Christleton in December 1963

and bread so that the less well-off would be able to share in
the general Christmas celebrations. But a few lucky souls
added to their larder by 'Yawning for a Cheshire cheese'. This,
presumably, involved the men rather than their wives and the
bizarre custom was on a par with gurning, that odd business
of pulling ugly faces through a horse-collar. When, after a
night's roistering and people began to yawn, the game was on.
The person who went on to yawn the widest and longest –
but *naturally*; no pretending was allowed – was declared the
winner and rewarded with a Cheshire cheese.

One group of people who may not have looked forward to
Christmas with the same degree of expectancy as others were
the farmers.

In the days when farmers took on their workers fresh each year
at Hiring Fairs the farmhands' year would run from 2 January (it
was considered unlucky to start work on New Year's Day) to the
next Boxing Day when their employment was automatically

terminated. From 27 December to 2 January farmers had to fend for themselves while their workforce whooped it up in the local inns. But in the Mobberly area farmers indulged in a little forward planning. During Mobberly Wakes, held every October, farmers would approach those labourers they wished to keep on for another year and ask them to stay on. Any workers not approached would know without asking that they were not being re-engaged.

A bit like professional footballers are treated today, really.

from
Thelwell's Brat Race

NORMAN THELWELL

Norman Thelwell, who hails from Tranmere in Birkenhead, is surely one of Britain's best-known artists. Who does not recognize a 'Thelwell pony' when they see one? It's a term which has passed into the English language.
His cartoons and humorous books have been published all over the world and in the course of a twenty-five year association with Punch *magazine he did over 1,500 drawings for them, including sixty front covers.*
The three cartoons which follow are but a snippet from Thelwell's Brat Race – *an hilarious pictorial commentary on the natural mischief, innate cunning, inherent savagery and general antisocial behaviour of the average child.*

A Cheshire Christmas

CHILDREN HAVE VERY DEFINITE OPINIONS ON WHAT IT IS THEY LIKE TO PLAY WITH

WHICH THEY QUICKLY LEARN HOW TO USE

76

AND THEY ADORE BEING GIVEN REAL TOOLS —

Stick-in-the-Mud

G.B. RADCLIFFE

*When Christmas comes around, the hunting season is at its
height and Boxing Day meets are always of special significance.
In 1959 Leslie Radcliffe, the well-known editor of the county
magazine* Cheshire Life, *invited his namesake, G.B. Radcliffe,
one of Cheshire's most illustrious names at that time, to
contribute to the Christmas issue of the magazine in a series
entitled 'One Crowded Hour . . . '.*

*Gershom Brainerd Radcliffe (known to his friends as 'GB')
was a man who excelled at everything he did. He was a highly
successful businessman who lived and also farmed at Tarvin. He
became a famous breeder, exhibitor and judge of Friesian cattle
and eventually President of the British Friesian Society. He was
an equally successful horse dealer and as a rider in his younger
days won many point-to-point races and hunter trials. A devout
Christian and a much sought-after lay preacher, Radcliffe also
became a very active President of Chester City Mission.*

*An enthusiastic hunting man, he was for ten years whipper-in
to the Cheshire Hounds. After the formation of the Cheshire
Forest Hunt he became whipper-in to that pack. One of the
horses which he sometimes rode to hounds was the Grand
National winner Russian Hero. When the following incident
took place he was in his eighty-second year.*

The Cheshire Forest were out hunting in Wirral and had met,
I recall, at the Yacht, Woodbank. The weather had been wet
and the going fairly heavy but I was whipping-in and

enjoying myself to the full, as I usually do. Hounds were drawing some kale at Backford, and I was sent to watch the bottom of the field. To get into a good position I had to cross a drain – typical of many in that part of the country. It was nothing of a jump – say, six feet across – but it was deep and full of black and most unpleasant looking sludge. My horse, Chance, took it in a stand, but at the moment of jumping the earth bank forming the lip of the ditch crumbled beneath him and instead of landing comfortably on the other side he came down half on the far bank and half nowhere at all.

Inevitably, I came off, falling on my back into the mud while the horse, equally inevitably, followed. That was nothing disastrous in itself – like any other hunting man I had been in the water and mud before – but on this occasion, Chance, having plunged down on top and trampled me a little (though without doing any real damage) stood aside me lengthways and began steadily to sink into the ooze. I was pinned helplessly beneath his belly.

I realized very quickly that if something, or someone, did not turn up pretty smartly I was going to end my days in a private little Passchendale of my own. I shouted as loud and as long as I could but it wasn't much of a shout, for when you're on your back at the bottom of a deep ditch half-stifled by black mud and a horse's belly, shouting is a very difficult accomplishment.

Fortunately, Mrs Bibby heard me and galloped across to see what was happening. As soon as she spotted me and realized the seriousness of the situation her shouts augmented mine to no mean purpose; a very good thing since by this time I was rapidly disappearing from sight as the weight of the horse drove me deeper into the slime, and it took all my efforts to breathe, much less to shout. Mrs Bibby's cries attracted Bobby O'Neill, the vet, who summed up the situation in a moment – or thought he did. 'What on earth are you hollering like that for?' he grinned, 'I'll get that horse out in no time.'

'It isn't the horse,' came the frightened reply, 'it's old G.B. – he's underneath!'

At that juncture the Master and a whipper-in rode up and a quick conference took place. It had to be quick, too, if I was ever to leave Wirral in any other transport than a hearse.

They dared not move Chance, for if they had, his plunging hooves would inevitably have landed on me and quite apart from forcing me to the bottom, would in all probability, have killed me, for at eighty-one one doesn't survive the buffetings that can be taken in youth. O'Neill held the horse's head to stop it making any fatal move and the Master got to one side of the ditch with the whipper-in on the other and grabbed my arms, but I was as tight as an oyster. I managed to get my head up for a moment, took a breath and said, 'when I push, you pull,' and began to kick like a frog while they heaved. Slowly, foot by foot, I emerged from beneath the horse's trembling forelegs like a cork from a bottle and ultimately half staggered, and was half dragged on to the ditch bank. The rest was easy. The horse was encouraged out and with much plunging and squelching joined me in safety.

Bobby O'Neill gave me a leg up and I remounted – at least I should have done so but the horse was covered with mud and when resaddled the slime underneath made the girth slippery and off I came again, with the saddle halfway round Chance's flank. Bobby resaddled him once again and this time I remounted uneventfully and galloped off towards my horse box two miles away. A follower travelling in a car with his girl groom recognized me – a considerable achievement in view of my condition – and sent the girl off with the horse while I travelled home in his car. On arrival I stripped in the yard as far as was decently possible and then made for a bath, philosophically drawn by my wife who, in a long married life, has too often seen me entering the house on gates and hurdles to panic. The water after the fourth rinse remained tolerably clear and I no longer smelt like a polecat. Indeed, except for a pair of rather sore eyes

for a few days owing to the acidity of the mud, that was the end of the matter and I spent the afternoon shopping with my wife in Chester and seeing a few of my friends.

They say the past life of a drowning man passes before him; either my life has been too long even to contemplate in the available time or the theory just doesn't work out in mud, for all I remember is the smell of the ditch, the unusual view I was getting of Chance's head from underneath – when I could get an eye open wide enough to see – and intense activity in an effort to co-operate with my rescuers.

This crowded hour was, more truly, crowded minutes. But believe me, when mud closes over your head and your position can only be marked by bubbles, minutes seem more like days than hours.

from

God's Providence House

MRS G. LINNAEUS BANKS

Mrs Banks was a novelist who was active in the latter years of the nineteenth century and the years prior to the First World War. While this book was inspired by the well-known building in Chester's Watergate Street much of the action takes place in the

A Cheshire Christmas

fictitious Grenville Grange, a large mansion rescued from near-dereliction, and located 'in a wild and desolate spot . . . between Chester and Parkgate, about half a mile west of Shotwick and considerably less than that distance from the River Dee'.
As was the traditional Christmas custom in most large houses the squire and his guests ventured below stairs to join in the staff celebrations.

The crowning glory of the kitchen was the mistletoe-bough, dependent from the centre of the raftered roof, on which the combined genius of men and maids had been concentrated. Not a bush to be spanned by a pair of long arms – three or four pairs could scarce have clasped it. There the mistletoe, with lip-like leaves kissing the waxen berries, held a prominent place, and tempted other lips to 'go and do likewise'. Then round the kissing emblem was clustered a circle of protecting holly with its bright red dots; round and above that the friendly ivy spread its glossy green. Apples and oranges, like golden balls, brightened and scented this radiant bough, like the famous fruit of the Hesperides; but there was no fiery dragon to guard the treasure – the prickly firs and holly alone stood sentry, and bristled their spears about it to keep off unkissed lips.

And there the Yule log spluttered and blazed and crackled, and the bright flame leaped about it in vain efforts to reach its hard heart, and make it glow through its whole length and breadth. But brighter and more cheery than the fire, or floor, or furniture, or platters, or pans, or winter berries, were the bright eyes and cheerful faces assembled there, in which all these bright things were reflected and grew brighter.

Dick and Ben, rejoicing in new smock frocks (Mrs Ford's Christmas gifts), with smoothly shaven chins, their lower limbs encased in grey woollen hose fresh from their sweethearts' knitting-pins, the heavy clogs in daily use replaced by their Sunday shoes, sat, one on each settle, as lords

of the place, laughing and joking with their fellows, the hinds, who in clean smock frocks, with wives or daughters also in holiday trim, had come, according to custom, to share the Christmas cheer and sports under their master's roof.

The three maid-servants, discarding their gingham or linsey gowns and grogram petticoats, were radiant as rainbows in dresses of brightly printed linen, tucked up behind to show the quilted camlet skirts. Their stays of coloured leather, stitched (like the men's smocks) in fanciful devices, confined over the bosom modest kerchiefs, white as their linen caps and aprons, or the snow without. Brass buckles spanned their insteps, calling attention to the neatly fitting stockings each girl's own deft fingers had produced.

In the corner nearest the fire, seated on a chair (to make room for which a settle had been pulled back), sat a Shotwick villager, little Job Last, who played the big fiddle in Shotwick Church. By dint of much cajolery on the part of Dick, Ben, and Peggy, who had been in a body to impress him that afternoon, he had been prevailed on to bring himself and his fiddle to the Grange. It had been a troublesome task (not the bringing of the fiddle, but the man), for he had a wholesome dread of all spirits that were not drinkable; but Peggy quenched his fears with the assurance that all ghosts or evil spirits lost their power on Christmas-eve, and only good angels were abroad; so there he was, ready to fiddle for their amusement and to feast for his own. They had brought him with them, lest his courage should fail.

When the party from the drawing room appeared at the door, Betty and Sally were bustling about concocting egged ale, whilst Peggy, with her back towards that entrance, stood before the fireplace, helping Dick to remove a heavy pot which hung suspended from the iron crane over the fire. This she said in answer to Mr Ford's question was, 'The mistletoe mash for th' pig'.

As they entered, the noise of tongues subsided only to rise in

In the eighteenth century roasting a Christmas joint was a dog's work!

clamorous greetings, in which 'Merry Christmas' and 'Happy New Year, an' many on 'em,' with the names of 'Mester and Mistress Ford, an' Miss Ailsie, an' Mester Yawood' (his name was pretty well known and his errand there also), blended in a confused chorus of good wishes and good will. The delighted yeoman, well pleased, went round from one to another, shaking each rough hand in turn, patting rosy cheeks, and complimenting matrons on their own good looks or those of their growing girls; inquiring after the children left at home, and the grannies left with them, with a cordiality which went straight to their homely hearts.

The egged ale being ready, it was handed round with roasted apples, toast and cake, and then a wooden trencher was produced, and a game of forfeits commenced, in which all took part; Mr Ford enjoying the fun as much as any of the lads and lasses about him. Even Mr Heywood condescended to dazzle the

eyes of the rustics like a brilliant meteor, and soon seemed very much at home amongst them; but the mistletoe-bough hung overhead, and Alice's lips looked tempting, cold as they were to him. As for Alice, powerless to resist, she resigned herself to the chances of the game with what composure she could; consoling herself that her compliance with Christmas usance could not be construed by Mr Heywood into open encouragement.

The trencher was turned, and first 'My lady went off in a very great hurry, and called for' Dick or Ben, or Mr Yawood or Hobnail, as the case might be, and 'My gentleman went off' in a similar hurry, and called for the petticoat that pleased him best; and so it went round, with sundry slips on the polished floor, and mirth and laughter in every corner. Then the forfeits were redeemed. Mrs Ford 'cried,' whilst Mr Ford awarded; and there was much scrambling and kissing, crushing of kerchiefs and rumpling of hair; the mistletoe-bough became denuded of its fruit, and amidst it all (as though the blindfolded awarder knew well what he was about and took a sly pleasure in mischief) Alice and Mr Heywood were called together under the mistletoe with a certainty and frequency never the result of chance, and no frowns of hers could dissipate the broad satisfaction visible in the countenances of both father and lover.

The last of the forfeits redeemed, more ale and cake went round; Job Last tuned his fiddle, and scraped away something that was meant for a country dance, and the motley guests stood up in couples. Mr and Mrs Ford leading, Alice and Mr Heywood following; then Dick and Peggy, Betty and Ben, Sally and some one else; and though Vestris would have shrugged his shoulders alike at figure and steps, the country dance was footed in true country fashion, and only finished when breath was short, and a fiddle string broke.

The ladies and gentlemen retired to supper in the long room when the dance was over, leaving the gratified servants to their own sports and feasting.

The Scribe's Tale

A Parable

LESLIE RADCLIFFE

The Christmas period, offering as it does a respite from the daily grind, is a time for reflection on the past and consideration of what is to come. One year this former editor of Cheshire Life *magazine gave deep thought to the fast-approaching day when his tenure of office would come to an end . . .*

It came to pass that on the Feast of Stephen in the twenty-seventh year of the reign of Elizabeth the Queen, I, Radcliffe the Scribe, gave thought unto that time, not then far distant, when my lord would cast me forth from his service to spend my days in idleness. Thus it was I addressed she who is my helpmeet, speaking straightly. 'Woman, what thinkest thou: hath not the hour come when we must needs part from our home of long-standing and purchase another of smaller compass wherein we may abide with lesser toil in the years remaining to us?' And she said, 'Thou speakest wisely, O my husband, for already my spirit groaneth within me at the burden our abode layeth upon me. But whither shall we go whereunto our children and our children's children may come to visit us? Let us not depart to live amongst strangers in a far off land.'

And so it fell out that we sought a soothsayer, a man devious in the arts of buying and selling homes of the afflicted. And he placed an inscription over against the house full of strange abbreviations which no man comprehendeth, seeking one who might purchase from us. In due season there came such a man,

A white Christmas at fifteenth-century Bramall Hall

much cumbered about with wife and children, who desired to purchase, though at a lesser cost than we were desirous of. But after debate a price was agreed betwixt us.

'Where shall now we go and what shall become of those chattels which have come down to us from our fathers?' waileth my wife. But soon there cometh a great press of merchants, full of guile, who spake to us with smooth tongues and carried away much of our heritage for payment of small sums of silver. And we went forth to wander over the face of the land seeking for a place where we might lay our heads. In due season we lighted upon a humble dwelling wherein there were but three bed-chambers, while behind lay a small garden in which grew apples and pears and divers other fruits of the earth, and for this we offered much gold lest, peradventure, another come and steal it from us.

Then called we upon our younger son, a youth cunning in the ways of architecture, who said to us, 'The room in which

ye abode in former times was nineteen cubits long but behold, this present room is but ten cubits. Ye must pull down the wall and build greater or else you and my mother will have strife as each trippeth over the feet of the other, and for as much as ye are both full of years, it is beholden upon me to plan also for a second privy to ease your climbing unto an upper room. This I will design, cutting off a portion of that area wherein lieth your chariot.' And this he did.

Then cometh my son unto me again, saying, 'I will go forth and find thee a builder' and in due season he returneth, giving me fair words. 'I have found a choice of two. The one is a master craftsman who will make promise of completion swiftly. But know you this: he will require payment of many shekels of gold. Now, if this be not to your comfort, there is one who cometh from across the sea and speaketh in a tongue which betrayeth him to be a Celt. He will do thy work for a lesser sum but as with all such, time meaneth but little and you must learn the ways of patience and fortitude.' My heart was heavy within me and I cried, 'We have not gold enough for a master builder. Let us employ the stranger within our gates that he may build as best he may.' And thus it was.

They digged the foundations like mighty men of valour, casting all that came out of the pit onto the grass of the lawn even unto the flowers and there was much distress in our hearts. They built then the two side walls of brick, plumbing with a plumb-line and levelling with a level. And behold, summer was now long overpast, and the voice of the turtle was no more heard in the land.

When the Feast of the Nativity was but four days off, they hewed out the end wall that formerly stood against the storm and naileth a veil of plastic over against the hole. Then cometh the chief of the builders unto me saying, 'Behold, now is come the holy day and we would fain return unto our own kindred that we may make merry, feasting and drinking poteen as did our fathers before us, and in seven days we will

return unto thy house.' And they would not take nay for an answer but cast down their implements and departed unto the far country from whence they had all come.

'Woe is me,' I cried, 'we are undone.' And verily this was well-nigh so, for the wind blew and the rain beat upon the house and the plastic veil stood in hazard of tearing asunder. 'Come,' said our children, 'come and celebrate Christmas with us and our little ones.' But we durst not, lest thieves break in to steal that little which we had left to us.

Unto my wife I said, 'Sorrow filleth my heart and I repent me of the arrangements we have made but there is nought we can do save await the return of these unprofitable servants. But be of good cheer, for privily we may use the new privy.'

And after ten days the labourers again entered our garden, their faces white and their hands shaking as do those of them that have the palsy. 'Give us drink,' they cried and gladly we plied them with black distillations of the coffee bean, whereupon they took up their tools of building and continued in the work until it were finished.

Truly the cost of the extension we were minded to build had increased mightily by leaps and bounds, leaping and bounding even as doth a hart upon the mountains. Nevertheless, when we had cast off the shaking sickness which had assailed us, we paid the price gladly and they departed. Whereupon, all being now fulfilled, we summoned our neighbours to a feast, and there were players playing upon the cornet, trombone, psaltery and saxophone and all kinds of music and our friends and family shouted with a great shout that the work was ended.

Therefore take heed, brethren, that when ye purchase an house and widen the confines thereof ye employ none but a master builder to build; and that he accomplish the work before Yuletide cometh, lest ye have great tribulation and through pneumonia are gathered prematurely to your fathers.

from

The English Notebooks

NATHANIEL HAWTHORNE

Nathaniel Hawthorne (1806–64), the famous American author of The Scarlet Letter *and* Tanglewood Tales, *was the US Consul in Liverpool from 1853 to 1857. For most of that time he lived on the Cheshire side of the River Mersey in a handsome villa (demolished a few years ago to make way for a bypass) in the private Rock Park, Rock Ferry, Birkenhead.*

He made the most of his stay in Britain and travelled widely but his attitude to England and all things English was somewhat ambivalent. He liked our ancient towns and cities, old churches and cathedrals, and the City of Chester held a special fascination for him. 'I must go again and again and again (he wrote) for I suppose there is not a more curious place in the world.'

He also admired some of our writers and poets but he was often highly critical of local civic officials and businessmen whom he often found to be duller than his compatriots. And he thought far too many were blatantly condescending to America and Americans and much resented that.

DECR 28th 1854

This is a most beautiful day of English winter; clear and bright, with the ground a little frozen, and the green grass, along the waysides at Rock Ferry, sprouting up through the frozen pools of yesterday's rain. England is forever green. On Christmas day, the children found wall-flowers, pansies, and pinks, in the garden; and we had a beautiful rose from the garden of the hotel – all grown in the .open air. Yet one is as sensible of the cold here, as in the zero atmosphere of America. The chief advantage of England is, that we are not tempted to heat our rooms to so unhealthy a point as in New England.

I think I have been happier, this Christmas, than ever before – by our own fireside, and with my wife and children about me. More content to enjoy what I had; less anxious for anything beyond it, in this life. My early life was perhaps a

No. 26 Rock Park,
the house occupied by
Nathaniel Hawthorne

good representation for the declining half of life, it having been such a blank that any possible thereafter would compare favorably with it. For a long, long while, I have occasionally been visited with a singular dream; and I have an impression that I have dreamed it, even since I have been in England. It is, that I am still at college – or, sometimes, even at School – and there is a sense that I have been there unconscionably long, and have quite failed to make such progress in life as my contemporaries have; and I seem to meet some of them with a feeling of shame and depression that broods over me, when I think of it, even at this moment. This dream, recurring all through these twenty or thirty years, must be one of the effects of that heavy seclusion in which I shut myself up, for twelve years, after leaving college, when everybody moved onward and left me behind. How strange that it should come now, when I may call myself famous, and prosperous! – when I am happy, too! – still that same dream of life hopelessly a failure!

DECEMBER 26TH, 1856, WEDNESDAY

On Christmas eve, and yesterday, there were little branches of mis[t]letoe hanging in several parts of our house, in the kitchen, the entries, the parlor, and the smoking room – suspended from the gas-fittings. The maids of the house did their utmost to entrap the gentlemen-boarders, old and young, under these privileged places, and there to kiss them, after which they were expected to pay a shilling. It is very queer, being customarily so respectful, that they should assume this licence now, absolutely trying to pull the gentlemen into the kitchen by main force, and kissing the harder and more abundantly, the more they were resisted. A little rosy-cheeked Scotch lass – at other times very modest – was the most active in this business. I doubt whether any gentleman but myself escaped. I heard old Mr Smith parleying with the maids last evening, and pleading his age; but he seems to have met with no mercy, for there was a sound of prodigious smacking,

immediately afterwards. Julian was assaulted, and fought most vigorously, but was outrageously kissed – receiving some scratches, moreover, in the conflict. The mis[t]letoe has white, wax-looking berries, and dull green leaves, with a parasitical stem.

Early in the morning of Christmas day, long before daylight, I heard music in the street, and a woman's voice, powerful and melodious, singing a Christmas hymn. Before bedtime, I presume one half of England, at a moderate calculation, was the worse for liquor. They are still a nation of beastly eaters and beastly drinkers; this tendency manifests itself at holiday time, though, for the rest of the year, it may be decently repressed. Their market-houses, at this season, show the national taste for heavy feeding; carcasses of prize oxen, immensely fat and bulky, fat sheep, with their woolly heads and tails still on, and stars and other devices ingeniously wrought on the quarters; fat pigs, adorned with flowers, like corpses of virgins; hares, wild fowl, geese, ducks, turkies [*sic*]; and green boughs and banners suspended about the stalls – and a great deal of dirt and griminess on the stone-floor of the market-house, and on the persons of the crowd.

There are some English whom I like – one or two for whom, I might almost say, I have an affection; – but still there is not the same union between us, as if they were Americans. A cold, thin medium intervenes betwixt our most intimate approaches. It puts me in mind of Alnaschar, when he went to bed with the princess, but placed the cold steel blade of his scimitar between. Perhaps, if I were at home, I might feel differently; but, in this foreign land, I can never forget the distinction between English and American.

JANUARY 1ST, 1856, TUESDAY

Last night, at Mrs Blodgett's, we sat up till twelve o'clock, to open the front door, and let the New Year in. After the coming guest was fairly in the house, the back door was to be opened,

to let the Old Year out; but I was tired, and did not wait for this latter ceremony. When the New Year made its entrance, there was a general shaking of hands, and one of the shipmasters said that it was customary to kiss the ladies all round; but, to my considerable satisfaction, we did not proceed to such extremity. There was singing in the streets; and many voices of people passing; and when twelve had struck, all the bells of the town, I believe, rang out together. I went up to bed, sad and lonely, and stepping into Julian's little room, wished him a happy New Year, as he slept, and many of them.

[To a cool observer, a country does not show to best advantage during a time of war. All its self-conceit is doubly visible, and, indeed, is sedulously kept uppermost by direct appeals to it. The country must be humbugged, in order to keep its courage up.]

Sentiment seems to me more abundant in middle-aged ladies, in England, than in the United States. I don't know how it may be with young ladies.

Snow can be fun – if you're young enough! Pupils of Bramhall County High School prove the point during the snows of December 1981

Women's Christmas Lunch

(with apologies to Longfellow)

DORA KENNEDY

Dora Kennedy (whose poem Run-up to Christmas *appears on page 6) lives in Heswall. She began writing poetry as a therapy after the loss of one of her daughters, followed by that of her husband. Many of her poems have been published in poetry and national magazines and some have been broadcast. This poem, inspired by a Townswomen's Guild Christmas luncheon party, is taken from her book* The Sheltering Coast *published by the National Poetry Foundation.*

On the edge of lower village,
By the mighty Dee the river,
Stands the home of Eleanora
Valued member of committee;
In the house are many comforts,
Carpets spread for all to tread on
Luxury seats for all to sit in.

On the fifteenth of December
When the sun had reached its zenith,
Aided by her friend and helper
From the Hermitage beside her
She made ready for the feasting;

A Cheshire Christmas

Soup in cauldron steaming, steaming,
Precious cut glass goblets gleaming,
Knives and forks and items sundry
For the coming of the hungry.

One by one the members gathered,
Each one bearing her own offering,
Many hours of preparation
Many thoughts and much discussion
Had been spent on these their efforts,
Trays they bore before them, laden,
Each one veiled in patterned napkin.

Came the mincepies, came the salads,
Beef and ham came, rolls and butter,
Sweets too numerous to mention,
At the last the famed Pavlova,
Quivering, quivering, as she bore it,
Dripping, dripping on her garment,
Almost lost before the feasting.

There they sat with well-filled glasses,
Wine from far across the water
Cheered them as they formed a circle
Clad in colours of the rainbow
Each one differing from the other.

Three times then they rose and gathered
Where the soup steamed gently, gently,
Where the food was waiting, waiting,
Where the famed Pavlova brooded,
Trifle, cheese and biscuits calling.

Red and gold, the Christmas crackers
Sparked, exploded as they pulled them,
Spilling hats and charms around them
Riddles that could not be fathomed,
And the talking and the laughter
Filled the room with warmth and gladness.

Coffee, and the feast was over;
Time to break the magic circle,
Each one took with her a portion
For the hungry waiting for them
In their houses waiting for them,
And the useful, mighty Hoover
With a noise, a sound like thunder
Cleared the crumbs from off the carpet,
Carpet spread for all to walk on.

Christmas skating in aid of charity on the frozen lake of Thornton
Manor, Thornton Hough, home of Viscount Leverhulme

from

An Exposition of the Creed

JOHN PEARSON

(Bishop of Chester 1673–86)

Bishop John Pearson has been described as 'the greatest theologian of his day,' while his book An Exposition of the Creed *is said to be 'the most perfect and complete production of English dogmatic theology'. He died in 1686 and was buried near the high altar in Chester Cathedral. The place of his burial remained forgotten until the grave was rediscovered by accident in 1841, whereupon the body was moved to the north transept. A massive monument surmounted by a recumbent effigy, designed by Sir Arthur Blomfield, was placed over it in 1863.*

I assent unto this as a most certain and infallible Truth, that there was a certain woman, known by the name of Mary, espoused unto Joseph of Nazareth, which before and after her Espousals was a pure and unspotted Virgin, and being and continuing in the same virginity, did by the operation of the Holy Ghost, conceive within her Womb the only-begotten son of God, and after the natural time of other women brought him forth as her first-born Son, continuing still a

most pure and immaculate Virgin; whereby the Saviour of the world was born of a Woman under the Law, without the least pretence of any original corruption, that he might deliver us from the guilt of sin; born of that Virgin which was of the house and lineage of David, that he might sit upon his throne, and rule for evermore.

We may delight and rejoice in the name of Jesus, as that in which all our happiness is involved. At his nativity an Angel from Heaven thus taught the Shepherds, the first witnesses of the blessed incarnation; 'Behold, I bring you good tidings of great joy, which shall be to all people. For unto you is born this day in the City of David, a Saviour which is Christ the Lord.' And what the Angel delivered at present, that the Prophet Isaiah, that old Evangelist, foretold at distance. When the people which walked in darkness should see a great

Where the snow lay deep and crisp and even two small Bramhall
boys made the most of it

light; when unto us a child should be born, unto us a son should be given then should there be joy before God, according to the joy of harvest.

The belief in Jesus ought to inflame our affection, to kindle our love towards him, engaging us to hate all things in respect of him, that is, so far as they are in opposition to him, or pretend to equal share of affection with him. The voice of the Church, in the language of Solomon, is, 'My love'.

from

Old Christmas

WASHINGTON IRVING

ILLUSTRATED BY RANDOLPH CALDECOTT

This is an evocation of an old-fashioned English Christmas as seen through the eyes of the famous American author of Rip Van Winkle. *While Irving had no direct connection with Cheshire he was, as a young man, in business only a mile away on the other side of the River Mersey in Liverpool. His book, however, was illustrated by Randolph Caldecott, one of the foremost illustrators of his day, and he was born in Chester. These extracts are reproduced as a vehicle for Caldecott's drawings since not to include something by him would be a grave sin of omission.*

THE CHRISTMAS DINNER

A sideboard was set out on which was a display of plate that might have vied (at least in variety) with Belshazzar's parade of the vessels of the temple; 'flagons, cans, cups, beakers, goblets, basins, and ewers'; the gorgeous utensils of good companionship, that had gradually accumulated through many generations of jovial housekeepers. Before these stood the two Yule candles beaming like two stars of the first magnitude; other lights were distributed in branches, and the whole array glittered like a firmament of silver.

We were ushered into this banqueting scene with the sound of minstrelsy, the old harper being seated on a stool beside the fireplace, and twanging his instrument with a vast deal more power than melody. Never did Christmas board display a more goodly and gracious assemblage of countenances: those who were not handsome were, at least, happy; and happiness is a rare improver of your hard favoured visage.

The parson said grace, which was not a short familiar one, such as is commonly addressed to the Deity, in these unceremonious days; but a long, courtly, well worded one of the ancient school. There was now a pause, as if something

was expected; when suddenly the butler entered the hall with some degree of bustle: he was attended by a servant on each side with a large wax light, and bore a silver dish, on which was an enormous pig's head decorated with rosemary, with a lemon in its mouth, which was placed with great formality at the head of the table. The moment this pageant made its appearance, the harper struck up a flourish; at the conclusion of which the young Oxonian, on receiving a hint from the squire, gave, with an air of the most comic gravity, an old carol, the first verse of which was as follows:

> Caput apri defero
> Reddens laudes Domino.
> The boar's head in hand bring I,
> With garlands gay and rosemary.
> I pray you all synge merily
> Qui estis in convivio.

Though prepared to witness many of these little eccentricities, from being apprised of the peculiar hobby of mine host; yet, I confess, the parade with which so odd a dish was introduced somewhat perplexed me, until I gathered from the conversation of the squire and the parson that it was meant to represent the bringing in of the boar's head: a dish formerly served up with much ceremony, and

the sound of minstrelsy and song, at great tables on Christmas day. 'I like the old custom,' said the squire, 'not merely because it is stately and pleasing in itself, but because it was observed at the College of Oxford, at which I was educated. When I hear the old song chanted, it brings to mind the time when I was young and gamesome – and the noble old college hall – and my fellow students loitering about in their black gowns; many of whom, poor lads, are now in their graves!'

The table was literally loaded with good cheer, and presented an epitome of country abundance, in this season of overflowing larders. A distinguished post was allotted to 'ancient sirloin,' as mine host termed it; being, as he added, 'the standard of old English hospitality, and a joint of goodly presence, and full of expectation'. There were several dishes quaintly decorated, and which had evidently something traditionary in their embellishments; but about which, as I did not like to appear over-curious, I asked no questions.

I could not however, but notice a pie, magnificently decorated with peacocks' feathers, in imitation of the tail of that bird, which overshadowed a considerable tract of the table. This the squire confessed, with some little hesitation, was a pheasant pie, though a peacock pie was certainly the most authentical; but there had been such a mortality among the peacocks this season, that he could not prevail upon himself to have one killed.

When the cloth was removed, the butler brought in a huge silver vessel of rare and curious workmanship, which he placed before the squire. Its appearance was hailed with acclamation; being the Wassail Bowl, so renowned in Christmas festivity. The contents had been prepared by the squire himself; for it was a beverage in the skilful mixture of which he particularly prided himself; alleging that it was too abstruse and complex for the comprehension of an ordinary servant. It was a potation, indeed, that might well make the heart of a toper leap within him; being composed of the richest and raciest wines, highly spiced and sweetened, with roasted apples bobbing about the surface.

The old gentleman's whole countenance beamed with a serene look of indwelling delight, as he stirred this mighty bowl. Having raised it to his lips, with a hearty wish of a merry Christmas to all present, he sent it brimming round the board, for every one to follow his example, according to the primitive style; pronouncing it 'the ancient fountain of good feeling, where all hearts met together'.

The Cathedral Lights Mystery

On 3 January 1837, the Chester Courant *reported that: 'A singular occurrence happened on Christmas Day during the afternoon service. The gas, with which the Cathedral is lighted, burnt so dimly that the congregation could see to read with difficulty, as Handel's fine anthem "The people that walked in darkness" commenced; till just at the conclusion of the passage, "have seen a great light", the gas burst forth again with great brilliancy, to the no small astonishment of all present; and it being Christmas Day, every part of the sacred edifice was crowded. The recitative "For behold darkness" was given with great effect by Mr Geo. Sherwin; and the grand chorus "For unto us a Child is born" was sung with great precision by the whole choir.*
The occurrence, we have no doubt, will long be remembered by those who witnessed it.'

There was a great gasp from the large congregation. Was it a minor miracle they had witnessed? Was it Divine intervention to add dramatic effect to the words? Could it be the spirit of Handel in a mischievous mood? Or was it just a cleverly contrived practical joke?

It was the talk of Chester for weeks and opinion was divided between the hand of God and 'collusion' on somebody's part with most educated opinion leaning towards the latter explanation.

But the distance between the Cathedral and Chester gasworks made 'collusion' an impossibility. When the gas suddenly dimmed as George Sherwin, a fine singer with a rich, powerful bass voice, had mouthed the words 'For behold darkness shall cover the earth' it was immediately assumed that there was a fault in the gas supply and a boy was told to run all the way to the gasworks and report it. But he could not have got very far before Mr Sherwin came to the words 'Upon them hath the light shined' and the gas shone forth again with what, it seemed to many, greater brilliance than ever.

No immediate explanation was forthcoming but forty years later the matter was raised in a letter to the December 1878 issue of *The Cheshire Sheaf*. It came from T. Hughes, a former choirboy, who wrote:

> Forty years ago and more my recollections go back to my schoolboy days – spent, the latter part of them, within the confines of the Cathedral – spent, four years of them, as a Foundationer of the Grammar School, and on the Choristers' Desk as a daily servitor in the Quire. Christmas in those days was, somehow or other, a different sort of thing to the Christmasses of my later experience; and I am willing to confess that, to my mind and memory, the former had a charm very much to be preferred to the make-believe latter.

We broke up for our holidays a few days previously. Our School Holidays of course I mean, for with us Choristers it signified a doubling of our church work – musical practices twice a day with our fiery tempered organist, Thomas Haylett – and with Ben Linney, George Sherwin, Sam Brown, Moss, Wilkinson and Humphreys, the then staff of lay vicars, whose performances were, to *my* mind, not so much behind their modern representatives as some folks would have us believe.

I remember well enough one Christmas afternoon – on which occasion the silver candlesticks at the altar were specially lighted to heighten the effect, and when the Quire was filled to overflowing as it always is on that particular day – all had gone well until Handel's glorious anthem 'For unto us a Child is born' with its prefatory recitatives, had just commenced. When Sherwin was reciting the words 'For behold darkness shall cover the earth' the supply of gas suddenly went down in a startling manner, and there was only just light enough for the singer to follow his part. A messenger was hurriedly despatched to the gasworks to notify the defect; but long before he could have reached there – just, indeed, as Sherwin had come to the words 'Upon them the Light shines' – the supply of gas suddenly returned and the anthem proceeded to its close without further incident or interruption.

This coincidence of time and the words of the anthem with the fall and rise of the gas made many people think that the accident was intentional; but from inquiries instituted at the time I am quite satisfied that such was not the case, and, indeed, the distance of the Cathedral from the source of gas supply precludes the possibility of any such collusion.

For all the forty years which had passed since the incident the letter from T. Hughes brought a response – and a full explanation.

It came from Robert Jones, MInstCE, the engineer in charge of the gasworks, written from his retirement home in Putney:

> The first intimation I got of the occurrence was from the late Mr Witter, a director of the Gas Company, who called next day to ascertain the cause. He asked 'Was there a preconcerted arrangement to produce the effect?'. Of course I scouted with indignation the idea of collusion, which my questioner honourably conceded; and being thus encouraged, I commenced by saying that, induced by the bright and genial state of the weather, and it being Christmas Day to boot, I took a stroll on the 'Navigation Cop'; that after walking a considerable distance I turned to retrace my steps, when to my horror I discovered that I had the key of the valve room of the gasworks in my pocket; and that, as the daylight was fast disappearing, the Cathedral would, to a moral certainty, be in a state of semi-darkness. I started at once to run, arrived at the gasworks and turned on the full supply of gas just as, it seems, Sherwin's fine and powerful voice reached those particular words – the previous 'darkness' being attributable alone to the want of sufficient gas in the main! Thus you have the whole 'bag of tricks' explained and what took place was simply an accidental coincidence having its origin in the forgetfulness of your present correspondent.

But many who were present in the Cathedral on that Christmas Day in 1836 went to their graves thinking otherwise.

The Christmas Ghost of Poulton Lancelyn

ANN LAKE

The story of a murdered nun, the suicide of the squire who attempted her seduction and the author's own ghostly experience within the ancient walls of a Wirral manor house.

This is the house. Of course it would have been incredible if the house hadn't a ghost. There are not many houses which are built on the site of a Saxon dwelling. Still fewer which have an unbroken record of ownership by the same family which has lived there since those pre-Domesday Book days. A family whose sons and daughters still bear their traditional Saxon names. Georgian and even Victorian additions have largely disguised the much older core. The atmosphere of the house is redolent of the long tale of its family's happenings, acts and emotions. Yet for all its long history the strongest impress of dramatic incident has been left not by the Saxon serf, Tudor tenant or Carolean cavalier but by the pathetic wraith of a little eighteenth-century nun.

This is the story. The American author, Nathaniel Hawthorne, when, as the US Consul in Liverpool he was living at Rock

Poulton Hall, Poulton Lancelyn, '. . . built on a site of a Saxon dwelling . . . it would have been incredible if the house hadn't a ghost'

Ferry, was shown the house in 1853 and was told a somewhat garbled account by its tenant-occupier. Hawthorne's version as it is published in one of his books varies in many important respects from the correct account which, as here recorded, is still told today by the owner-descendant of the chief actor.

One snowy Christmas late in the eighteenth century, a nun was sent from the convent in Chester to the sister convent in Birkenhead. The girl (who was young and beautiful) had a terrifying journey. The short day ended early and a violent blizzard made the darkness yet more fearful. The road from Chester to Birkenhead was long and with each change of horses the coachman's anxiety mounted. The vehicle was

heavily laden with Christmas travellers and their baggage; all longing to reach their welcoming firesides. The roads were already thick with snow through which the horses, blinded by the whirling flakes, laboured desperately to drag the weighty stage coach. But in spite of all their efforts and the coachman's skill, on a particularly lonely stretch of road there was a sudden sickening lurch, the plunging horses slipped on the icy road and with a crash the great coach overturned spilling its occupants into the deep drift and the dreadful loneliness of the dark storm.

The passengers were forced to make their way on foot in search of any shelter they could find. All were shocked and distressed; probably some were injured. Perhaps they were all too distracted and frightened to give a thought to the nun who, travelling alone, had held no converse with the other passengers. They may not even have noticed whether she was there. She set off on foot quite alone and must have struggled a considerable distance through the storm from the scene of the accident in her anxiety to reach her destination. At last, when her strength was almost gone, she saw a light shining from the window of a large house. Hopeful that she would at least find shelter till morning and perhaps with daylight, some means of conveyance to Birkenhead so that she might still be in time for the Christmas Mass, she knocked at the door and begged admittance.

It so happened that the old hall where she had sought refuge was at that time occupied by a member of the family whose reputation was particularly unsavoury. Perhaps the most striking commentary on his character is that many years after the man was dead his great grandson (always known in the family as 'the Old Squire') invariably *spat* if obliged to mention the name of his reprobate ancestor! The rogue's last actions proved the justification for his descendant's aversion. For when he realized that his involuntary guest was a young

lovely and unprotected woman, neither her youth, virginity nor religious calling weighed one jot with him. He employed every wile he could conjure up to seduce her. At last, finding all unavailing, he turned to force. Locking her in an upstairs room, he told her brutally that she could either submit or starve to death. Inevitably she was faithful to her vows; he unlocked the door one day to find her dead of cold and starvation.

It could have been some belated stab of shame or remorse which drove him next door to his library where he hanged himself. The rape, or attempted rape and certain murder of any young girl is not lightly forgotten. When the victim has been a nun it is not surprising that an evergreen (or, rather, ever-black!) memory of the event should remain in the family traditions. The library with its evil associations gradually fell into disuse and (on account of the great value of the books) was kept locked.

This is what subsequently happened. Some 150 years later when even 'the Old Squire' had been succeeded by *his* grandson, a schoolfriend of the 'Major's' wife (as the 'new' squire was known) came to stay at the Hall. This lady, who had not seen her friend for many years, knew nothing at all about the history of the house or family of her friend's husband. As she was greatly interested in old houses, the Major offered to show her the library, being a room of very unusual character. This room, while still retaining all its striking features, had now been transformed by the Major's son into a charming and cheerful study.

The Major had just unlocked the door and ushered his guest inside when he was called to the telephone. He returned some minutes later to find the visitor (who was an experienced psychic investigator) sitting clasping her head in her hands in a distracted manner. Greatly disturbed, he asked

The Queen Anne library built by Thomas Green in about 1710. It was here that Squire Joseph hanged himself

if she were ill. She replied she was in acute distress as she had reacted to the fact that someone had killed themselves in the room just where she was sitting.

Nor was this the end of the tale. A few years later, my husband and I were taken to dinner at the Hall. Neither of us knew anything whatever of our hosts or their background.

On arrival a maid took me up to a bedroom to leave my wrap. As I came out of the room I met my hostess who asked me to wait a few moments while she gave some instructions to the nursery so that we could go down together. Left alone, and hesitating whether to follow my hostess or return to the bedroom, I stepped aside into a

recess with two doors. Immediately I was overwhelmed by an almost paralysing sensation of terror and a driving urgency at all costs to escape from the house. Without conscious volition I ran along the passage and down the stairs, only coming to the realisation of what I had done when I found myself in the lighted hall. After more than thirty years the recollection is still vividly with me of the terrible sense of imprisonment and evil; the frantic necessity to escape from an appalling doom; the blinding terror and despair.

Only many years after, through intimacy with the family, did I learn the story and that I had been standing between the doors of the rooms which had witnessed the deaths of the nun and her persecutor.

So was it the ghost of the nun, or of the 'Wicked Squire'; or was it the overpowering sense of the crime and tragedy itself which still left that haunting impress of horror to grip the unwary or psychic visitor with its petrifying chill? Whichever it may have been the houseful of lovely children who are now enjoying their heritage in the old house should, especially at the Christmas season, finally dispel any lingering baleful influence which may have been imprinted there, with the best of all antidotes; joy and love.

Christmas at Lyme

DAME LILIAN BROMLEY DAVENPORT

*Another memory of a Christmas spent at Lyme Park, this time
by an aunt of the author of* Treasure on Earth. *Dame Lilian
was in her eighties when she wrote this account and by
coincidence was probably doing so around the time Mrs
Sandeman was writing her book. Both were looking back to
those years between the end of the last century and the outbreak
of the First World War.
The Bromley Davenport family of Capesthorne Hall near
Macclesfield can trace their descent directly from the Saxon,
Onmus de Davenporte. Dame Lilian (1878–1972) was
the grandmother of the present head of the family, Mr
William Bromley Davenport, who is Cheshire's Lord
Lieutenant.*

Lady Newton was my husband's sister and before the First
World War it was our custom to spend Christmas at Lyme.
This was no hasty, after-breakfast drive in a car from
Capesthorne to Disley and return in the small hours of Boxing
Day, but a well-planned and protracted visitation extending
over the best part of a fortnight.

The luggage – a considerable amount – was piled into an
estate cart early in the morning and plodded steadily away,
accompanied by estate staff on foot, while we would travel
later in the day by carriage, to arrive about tea time.

Today, visitors to Lyme almost exclusively use the main
drive leading from the Stockport–Buxton road, but by far the

loveliest approach has always been the way we came – up through Purse Fields. Eight hundred feet up and on an incomparable site, few houses can vie with the magnificence of its setting. I can still sense the sway of the carriage and the faint squeak of crisp snow beneath the wheels, the horses' hoof-beats deadened by the white carpet on the road. A whisp of flakes would be caught on an occasional flurry of wind and from time to time gaunt trees released their burden of snow which fell with a subdued thud through the lower branches until it lost its identity on the ground beneath. It was a world of breathless, almost tangible, silence.

Then the great Palladian mass of Lyme would appear, its windows golden with welcoming lights. The carriage would sweep into the porch where the hall porter and the two footmen would be waiting and, hovering behind, the surprising figure of the immaculate Truelove, Lord Newton's butler. Surprising, since he wore a beard impeccably trimmed after the manner of King Edward VII. With that majestic deference only achieved by perfectly trained servants he would escort us across the courtyard and up the steps into the hall, where coats would be shed before we climbed a short flight of stairs to the saloon where our hostess would be waiting to greet us.

Today, the saloon is still beautiful and will always remain so as long as Grinling Gibbons' superb carving in yellow pearwood survives. But it is now no more than a pale shadow of its former glory. Here was elegance and comfort at its height. The walls were glowing cedar wood while pairs of Corinthian pilasters divided the long panels, each decorated with swags of carving. The Italian gilt scroll work of the ceiling looked down on lovely furniture and delicate Dresden and Chelsea china. The electric lights – for the house generated its own supply – shone on yellow damask curtains and, reflecting in the great mirror opposite the door, seemed to invest the room with a golden haze.

Christmas at Lyme was celebrated in the early days of the century with almost feudal splendour. The running of the great house and the comfort of those who lived in it virtually rested with three people – Truelove, who preferred the title of steward to that of butler, Mrs Campbell, the housekeeper, and Monsieur Peres, the chef. Round these three revolved the whole staff and, to a greater degree than perhaps they realised, their employers. Their lightest word to the lower servants and they ruled with the composure of royalty. In this modern world they would be an anachronism and yet tears came into my eyes in the servants' hall when the glory eventually passed away. Although everyone had a place in the scheme of things, and knew it, there was far more of a family attitude than we can understand in this generation.

On Christmas Eve would take place a typically feudal custom, but one greatly enjoyed and appreciated. Truelove would present himself at the saloon door to announce that the men were waiting below and Lady Newton would gather her children and those guests who had a mind to assist and make for the kitchen. The passage between this and the servants' hall would be lined by the men of the estate. Lady Newton would stand at a small table surrounded by her family and flanked by innumerable joints of meat, while Truelove would call the roll. As each man came to the table he would spread out a napkin and into it would be placed a joint, varying in size according to his family needs, and Lady Newton would knot the cloth over the top, wishing the recipients a happy Christmas and then repeating the formula for the next man. They came strictly in order of precedence, starting with the coachman, the head gardener, the clerks of works, the head keeper and so on, and by the time the last man had been served it was a full hour nearer Christmas Day.

The twenty-fifth of December began early, with the arrival of the church choir, who quite voluntarily trudged up from

the village and, after a breakfast in the servants' hall, gathered in the courtyard and sang carols to the awakening guests. This was followed in due course by the general exodus of the house party, some on foot and some by carriage to the village church for Christmas service.

Presents, except the more intimate family ones, were piled upon the billiards table in the vast Long Gallery in which stood a tree of perfect symmetry decorated as I have never seen one before or since. This again was the work of Truelove who was a real artist, even adding extra branches to the tree where a sense of balance required it.

After the gifts came dinner, set out in the Georgian dining room with the table extending almost its entire length. The footmen wore black knee breeches on special occasions such as this and at Christmas served a majestic meal on silver plates, brought out for the occasion, with tireless efficiency to the twenty or thirty guests.

After Christmas came the theatricals, always a welcome feature in days before the present blasé approach to entertainment engendered by easy travel, films, radio and television. These lasted three evenings – the first was really a dress rehearsal to which came all the staff, the next night the élite of the town and country gathered and at the last performance gathered all the tenants and villagers. Amateur the performances may have been, but they achieved a remarkably high standard nevertheless, and were savoured to the full.

And so the days would go by with shooting parties, squash, skating and the like until New Year's Eve when the final great night of the visit took place – the Servants' Ball.

This was an occasion with considerable panache, held above the stairs in the large hall. The band were positioned on a platform at one end and then a side door would open and Truelove would emerge with Mrs Campbell on his arm followed by all the other servants (once more, strictly in order of

precedence). Each servant was allowed to invite one friend and when all were assembled, together with the house party and the senior outside staff, the large hall was very comfortably filled.

Invariably the dance began with the same melody and invariably Lady Newton set the pace by taking the opening dance with the coachman as partner – the honour really belonged to Truelove but, as a devout Plymouth Brother, he disapproved of dancing and was excused. Lord Newton danced with Mrs Campbell and other members of the family with senior servants. The rest of us partnered whom we liked. At midnight Truelove would reappear for the singing of Auld Lang Syne, after which Lord and Lady Newton would appear in the 'secret' cavity behind the picture on the Hall wall and wish all the dancers a Happy New Year. Then the house guests would extricate themselves and make for bed leaving the hall to the staff who danced on until five in the morning. Many a pale-faced housemaid changed out of her dance frock into uniform and went straight on duty on New Year's Day.

All this belonged to a world now gone forever. Lyme still stands and echoes to the voice of throngs of people, but they are no longer house guests or servants. Each has paid his half-crown to Stockport Corporation and the only rules of precedence belong to him who reaches the door first. In all fairness, the Corporation do a very good job and are undoubtedly proud of the great house they administer under the National Trust. They are prepared, in fact, to add a few pence to the rates without a murmur, to help in the upkeep of this beautiful responsibility. But it can never be the same without a family living within the walls – even Lyme's distinctive smell, compounded largely of old timber, bees-wax and turpentine, has faded for ever.

The clock of history cannot be put back, and perhaps it is better so, but those who have lived to experience the delights of a more opulent age are fortunate in having wonderful memories of a way of life which can never again return.

from

Bishop's Brew

THE RIGHT REVEREND RONALD BROWN

(Bishop of Birkenhead)

*When the Archbishop of Canterbury asked the Diocese of Chester
to raise £650,000 for his Church Urban Fund the Bishop of
Chester suggested that the clergy and churchgoers of the diocese
should try to raise the money by means of sponsored events.
Bishops were not excluded from the exercise and the Right
Reverend Ronald Brown, the then Bishop of Birkenhead,
conceived the idea of asking the diocesan clergymen to
contribute to an anthology of clerical jokes and anecdotes.
The resulting book, called* Bishop's Brew, *was first
published in hardback in 1989 and was such a success that
it was reprinted three times. Sadly, however, before a single
penny in royalties had been paid the publisher went into
liquidation. But two years later Arthur James Limited
republished the book in paperback and seven further
reprintings later it is still selling well.*

It was the Christmas season and the vicar decided to ask the
children what difference it would make if Christ had not been
born. There were plenty of expected answers – no Christmas
tree, no presents, no nativity play, and so on. After the service
one ten-year-old boy sidled up to the vicar and said: 'If Jesus
hadn't been born, you'd be out of a job'.

A Christmas nativity play was being arranged. The boy chosen to take the part of Joseph was too small for the costume so he was asked to be the innkeeper instead. He did not like the change. On the night Mary and Joseph knocked on the door of the inn Joseph said: 'May we come in?'. The innkeeper replied: 'Mary can but you can b. . . . . off'.

An American bishop told this story at a Lambeth conference. A young priest wished to give a warning to his congregation during Advent. He did not, however, want to make it too emphatic and so eventually his message came out as follows: 'My brethren, if we repent – more or less – and if we confess – to a certain extent – we shall be saved – as it were'.

★

The vicar was catechizing the kindergarten about the Christian year. 'And what happened on Christmas Day?' he asked brightly. A small boy, aged five, replied solemnly: 'Daddy was sick on the stairs'.

from

Homage to Cheshire

HEDLEY LUCAS

*If ever a man loved Cheshire it was Hedley Lucas,
Barrister of Gray's Inn, Master of the Manchester Royal
Exchange, one-time Chief Executive of the Voluntary
Hospital Service but, above all, a poet. His deep love for his
native county manifested itself in scores of poems which
flowed effortlessly from his pen on every subject under the
Cheshire sun – its topography and geography; its history
and traditions; its heroes and its heroines; its legends and
its labours; its characters and the seasons of the year. His
fertile mind swept the county like some giant radar beam –
from Birkenhead to Bollington, from Malpas to
Macclesfield, omitting nothing.
The two poems which follow are taken from the
sixth edition of his (most appropriately titled)
Homage To Cheshire, published in 1960 with each
successive edition being an enlargement of the
preceding one.*

A CHESHIRE CHRISTMAS CAROL

Earth's black and white,
Bare land, frost-light,
Sing joyously
For God's Baby.

A Cheshire Christmas

By mere and hill,
On plain, goodwill,
Sing joyously
As Christ you see.
A savour town,
A silken gown,
Sing joyously,
Mary, Mother she.
True common ways,
For work be praise,
Sing joyously,
As Joseph be.

The high and low,
And wise, aglow,
Sing joyously,
God's love the key.
The farm and field
For pasture's yield,
Sing joyously,
A manger see.
On gentle stream
There floats a dream,
Sing joyously,
High destiny.
Within a wood
The deathless good,
Sing joyously,
Adorn the tree.
By church man's blest
When God is quest,
Sing joyously,
Christmas is He.

CHRISTMAS – EASTER

No room at the inn,
Yet God a temple made
For man to worship in,
Love on its altar laid.
There the heart adores
Christ the Saviour Child
Best when it restores
God as the domiciled.

The time is set for joy's ascent,
Beauty is raised unto the light,
The Lord has Risen from Deep Descent,
And man would make earth's road more bright.
So heart rejoices, for breaks the day
That lifts the soul to life anew,
And from the depth of man's dismay
A quiet, gleaming faith anew.

In the bleak midwinter of 1964 Redesmere was frozen solid

125

from

God's Providence House

MRS G. LINNAEUS BANKS

*This second extract from Mrs Banks' novel describes the
Christmas dinner and festivities 'upstairs' where the servants
were given a place at the table along with the family and
guests.*

In the long parlour two or more tables had been joined to
supply a board of sufficient length for host and hostess,
guests gentle and simple, servants both men and maids, to
sit down and dine together, and that without so much as the
salt cellar distinction of feudal times. True, the servants
occupied the end nearest to the kitchen, but for convenience,
not distinction; while Mrs Wright and her daughter held
the post of honour (if such there were) on either side of Mr
Ford, in the light of the large bay window; Mr Dutton not
being driven far from his lady-love. With the double design
of marking the relation between Alice and Mr Heywood,
and placing all at the festive board that day on an equal
footing, Michael had contrived to seat them opposite to each
other, midway down the table, in the midst of the villagers,
a distinction as agreeable to Robert as it was annoying and
painful to her.

On the glossy white napery, kept in lavender for such solemn occasions, and on the best willow pattern dinner service, was spread a bountiful supply of Christmas dainties. The fat porker killed during the past week furnished the boar's head, which, with rosemary in eyes and ears, and a lemon in its jaws, occupied the centre of the table, as the chief dish of the day; notwithstanding the noble presence of sirloin, or turkey, or goose, or Christmas pie, or the scarcely less important matters of fowls and game. It is needless to recount the fabulous piles of vegetables that disappeared, as concomitants of these savouries, when the green handled two-pronged knives and forks began to rattle over the well supplied plates. Nor would it be wise or fair to measure all the home-brewed ale that leapt and frothed from huge cans into glass, silver, or pewter that day. A savoury steam filled the large apartment, pervaded with a combination of appetizing odours, very grateful to the olfactory organs, when the other senses were as agreeably employed.

As the carvers began to weary of their task, the green hafted knives were plied less sedulously, and as the home-brewed vanished in capacious libations, tongues were loosened, and, with the potent spell of the season upon them, conversation became merry and unrestrained. Then Mrs Ford and her maids removed the ruins to replace them with mince pies, custard, and a mammoth plum pudding, crowned with holly, and blazing in a sea of burnt brandy. Cakes, jellies, and winter fruits followed home-made wines, and more ale filling up the measures of the Christmas feast, which had been already warmed and spiced with a genial, hearty welcome such as only large, open, honest Christmas hearts like theirs could give.

But remnants, china, glass, and tables removed, the polished oak floor denuded of its centre carpet, every crumb swept away, and the entertainment branched off in a fresh

direction. Mr Ford, beaming and jolly, proposed a song, easy to propose, not so easy to obtain. After much persuasion, Miss Wright seated herself; at Alice's old harpsichord, and astonished the ears of the rustics with a variety of most extraordinary shakes and quavers. Alice also sang, accompanying herself; then, with some little reluctance, played an accompaniment for Mr Heywood while he did his best to sing, 'Had I a heart for falsehood framed,' and pointed his somewhat unmusical effort with very tender and significant glances at the shy musician.

Next Phœbe – who had picked up music at school (as she had picked up many other things), from her schoolmates, who gave her secret lessons in return for little outdoor favours – Phœbe ran her little fingers over the keys, and sweetly warbled the old ballad, 'Love me little, love me long,' so archly, she drove the two enraptured swains to deeper depths of distraction, and won from tame Mr Dutton such looks of undisguised admiration as brought a curl of scorn on the lip of his fair inamorata. Mr Ford now insisted on a song from Miles; whereupon Job Last, after setting all sensitive teeth on edge with tuning his fiddle, scraped the melody of a somewhat pathetic ballad, setting forth the cruelty of father, mother, sister, and brother, and of things animate and inanimate, which sundry and severally had ended in driving somebody's 'true love to sea' – a lachrymose ditty articulated by Miles in true ballad fashion.

Matthew, then, not to be outdone in the presence of Phœbe, bespoke the services of Job, apparently used to the office, and sung out in a voice like the roar of his own forge, 'A wealthy young squoire in Tamworth did dwell,' lingering with peculiar gusto on the final choice of the young lady of the ballad betwixt her two lovers. It was now Mr Ford's turn, and with palpable indication of sly humour in his eye, at the selection he had made of a theme, he trolled out in genuine

earnestness, 'There was a jolly miller lived on the river Dee'. In due order, the fair-haired Mr Dutton joined the fair Miss Wright in a duet, abounding in 'loves' and 'doves,' 'hearts' and 'darts,' 'fears' and 'tears,' sentimentally arranged for the especial behoof of lackadaisical lovers of both sexes. Mr Heywood, again appealed to, essayed 'The Thorn', but made a sad break down; and then, while one of the nameless villagers caused the room to ring again with a grand 'Tol-de-rol' chorus, in which everybody joined, or affected to join, tea was introduced for the daintier guests, and buttermilk and more ale supplied for less luxurious palates.

A-beagling We Will Go!

The Royal Rock Beagles of Wirral can lay claim to being the oldest surviving beagle pack in England. Their one-hundredth hunting season was celebrated with a grand ball in Chester in 1951 but their origins date back to 1845. In that year a number of Rock Ferry gentlemen met at the home of Mr Christopher Rawson Jnr 'to form a subscription pack of Beagles for the purpose of hunting hounds over the Hundred of Wirral'.

The pack takes its name from the Royal Rock Hotel on the edge of the Mersey at Rock Ferry where the first kennels were established. Except for a forced break during each of the two

world wars the beagles hunted hares across the farmlands and fields of the Wirral Peninsula and since it was a foot hunt crowds of followers were always attracted to the scene – especially on Boxing Day.

In the years following the end of the Second World War the Boxing Day meet was always on the village green in Willaston – a circumstance not unconnected with the fact that Willaston was the village where the then Master resided. The meet soon became established as a popular Boxing Day outing for scores of Wirral families seeking a novel and pleasurable way of working off the excesses of the previous day.

The pack still hunts today but Wirral is no longer their happy hunting ground. The insidious development of the peninsula and, not least, the bisecting of their territory by the

The Royal Rock Beagles meet on the green at Willaston-in-Wirral, Boxing Day 1975

mid-Wirral M53 motorway brought about a move to the still verdant countryside of North Wales.

This newspaper report of a Boxing Day meet at Willaston in the 1970s suggests that it is not the catching of a hare which counts so much as the chase and the taking part. And patently, everyone – hunt subscribers and the throng of followers alike – had a splendidly invigorating time.

The Royal Rock Beagles have been busy over the Christmas period. On Christmas Eve, at Ince, they caught a hare which sat too tight and then they went on to the marshlands by the Manchester Ship Canal where hares abounded and hounds were stopped after they had split into three lots.

Boxing Day was just as it should be, with hosts of friends, hosts of people, and plenty of activity in the field.

On the way to the Royal Rock at Willaston we visited our friends in the Cheshire Forest Hunt at Burton. A mounted field of more than a hundred foxhunters, including many young, was followed by hundreds of foot and car followers. Among a number of representatives of Wirral farming families, Mrs John Scott of East Farm, Caldy crossroads, was riding an outstandingly handsome hunter.

At Willaston another crowd, entirely foot-slogging, was assembling for the beagles. Hounds moved off with Rodney Symonds, our new huntsman, carrying the horn and the Master, Terence Harvey, in overall charge. The column of followers along Mill Lane, including every age group from seventy-plus to five-minus, was at least half a mile long, and must have reached a thousand.

Many did not leave the lane, but those who did were soon sorted into runners and walkers when hounds put up a hare on Mr Tedstone's Raby House Farm, burst into

full cry, and went away towards the Clatterbridge Road and then over it and still further on, till they checked near the water tower at Hinderton.

Then they returned to Willaston country and spent the rest of the day there with several hares afoot, until they were stopped when scent deteriorated.

On the way back we met a party of foxhunters hacking home, among them Mr Fred Lancaster of Badger's Rake Farm, who has done so much for sport in Wirral.

'Not much scent outside cover,' they said. Well, what did it matter? It was Boxing Day. They looked happy, and we were certainly happy – all the more so for this meeting of friends at the end of the day in the dreamy half-light of the mid-winter's afternoon.

W.V.S.

from

Treasure on Earth

PHYLLIS ELINOR SANDEMAN

This second extract from Treasure on Earth *finds young Phyllis up in her bedroom on the eve of the great day 'thinking her Christmas thoughts'.*

After Louisa had left her, Phyllis sat for a while in the old plush-covered armchair by the fire thinking her Christmas thoughts.

Her red-curtained bed waited invitingly with the sheet turned down. She had placed it along the wall so that the curtains spread over head and foot gave it a tent-like appearance. Her stocking hung at the bed-foot, but it was now little more than a symbol, a traditional rite to be observed, and it was never filled with anything more exciting than nuts, almonds and raisins, sweets and tangerines. Last year though wide awake she had laid quietly feigning sleep whilst Father Christmas in the guise of Mrs Campbell entered rather noisily, breathing rather heavily and groping about in the dark, spilling several nuts in the process, filled her stocking and retired again.

To the right of the door stood the little glass-fronted cabinet made for her in the Vyne workshop to hold her collection of Goss china. On the top of the Victorian wardrobe sat the two early Victorian dolls, a boy and a girl with china faces, dressed in heavy, dark-coloured clothes. The Jacobean chest-of-drawers was a twin to the one in the Oak Room;

133

'The great Palladian mass of Lyme . . .'

several handles had been off it for a long time; and on the wall behind her, tilted forward at an angle, hung a long, very narrow cheval glass; there was one exactly like it in her mother's bedroom.

Phyllis loved her room, as indeed she did every room at Vyne. She could have identified any one of them if led into it blindfold by its individual smell. The 'Room' (occupied by Truelove, the butler) smelt of beer and coconut matting, the still-room of hot cakes and scones, the schoolroom was a blend of Mike, Lady, ink and Fräulein's cough drops. Her father's study smelt of tobacco, Harris tweed and Russian leather; her mother's boudoir of violets and sealing wax. The drawing room had the most distinctive smell of all and the hardest to define – it seemed to be composed of spices, pot-pourri, beeswax and the past. The combined essence of all these individual scents which made the peculiar fragrance belonging to Vyne was one of the first things one noticed on returning there from London, and most of all at Easter.

They would drive up through the park from the station, mounting gradually all the time, and Sir Thomas would

remark that the grass had not yet started to grow. But Phyllis could discern the look and smell of Easter in the keen northern air, would notice the green spikes of the daffodils with here and there a narrow golden bud – for spring came late to Vyne. They would turn in at the forecourt gates, the dogs leaping up to welcome them as they got out. John's face above his yellow striped waist-coat would be ruddy and smiling, and Mrs Campbell would be there too.

But after she had greeted them, Phyllis would rush, not out to the garden, but up the back stairs, closely followed by Lady, to her dear waiting bedroom, and the sweet fresh smell of it after London was not the least of her joys. So it must always have been – its sons and daughters yearning for it when they were away. 'Dear Vyne – Sweet Vyne,' they wrote in that crabbed writing Lady Vyne was to risk her eyesight in deciphering. 'My dearest Deare,' wrote Richard Vayne, the Member of Parliament, from Charles II's London to his wife at Vyne, 'would that I were at home with thee and the deare brats.' And just so today, the Vaynes when in London yearned for their northern home.

Fräulein was playing Wagner's 'Fire Music' in the adjoining schoolroom. Phyllis liked to hear it after she had gone to bed; the sound of the piano was friendly and comforting if, as did not often happen now, her night fears were upon her.

Slowly and at leisure she began her bedtime toilet. She liked the mottled blue and white of her jug and basin, simulating marble, but Lettice had a prettier set with a pattern of acorns round the edges. The brown hot water can always smelt of hot enamel and flakes of it sometimes came off in the water.

She wondered whether Althea was asleep by now or lying awake joyfully anticipating the morrow. It must be wonderful to be Althea, but if by some magic they could exchange personalities she knew that she would never do so.

Tomorrow she would be moving in a maze of enchantment through the dance drama of Christmas, that drama in which the setting played so great a part. Waking in the twilight of the winter's morning, waiting for the singing in the courtyard, the herald of the day's delights. Breakfast and the exchange of small gifts. The visit to her parents' rooms together with her brothers and sisters to give them their joint offerings. Then the drive down through the white park to the old church – the familiar Christmas service – 'And it came to pass in those days that there went out a decree from Caesar Augustus, that all the world should be taxed'. A very short sermon from Mr Hunt and the lovely Christmas hymns. Home again for luncheon, with the table stretching almost the whole length of the big room. The boar's head on the sideboard. The joking and fooling in the library. Then out-of-doors for a little exercise, snowballing perhaps if there was enough snow, then in again to change for tea in the dining room with lovely iced cakes and crackers. And then the joyous chattering throng climbing the stairs to the Long Gallery.

And there would stand the great shimmering blazing tree, the only light in the room except the fire, and beside it the bran tub, so full that some of the packages were not quite submerged, and beyond the radius of the tree's light the great long room stretching away into the shadows.

They would begin by drawing out the presents one at a time. 'Phyllis, with love from Papa and Mamma.' 'Althea, with love from Uncle Tom and Aunt Evy.' But very soon the tempo would quicken, till they were all pulling them out together. It would seem to go on for ages. And then there was the almost equal delight of examining one's own and other people's presents and playing with them, and then the little pause before it was time to get ready for dinner. There seemed no end to the delights, and all the time and independent of all

this that strange, indescribable feeling in the air which only came at Christmas. 'Oh, Heaven, Heaven!' thought Phyllis, getting ready for bed.

One day (and this was hard to believe) she would be an old woman and would have to die. One hoped at death to go to one's true home. She was past the stage when one verse in the hymn 'There's a Friend for Little Children' evoked visions of gold crowns kept in the nursery cupboard ('Nana, can I wear my crown this morning?'). But her childish mind could only take in purely anthropomorphic images. Life in heaven must be life at Vyne with all the highspots of delight eternally repeated and prolonged, with all the people she knew and loved around her, and God and Son sometimes coming over the moors to visit them walking on the water.

Phyllis resolved to be up and waiting for the carol singers when they came in the morning. Were they not the herald angels of whom they would afterwards be singing in church, the overture to the Christmas drama, the bringers of the glad tidings of great joy? There was not long to wait now before the drama would begin – the curtain was trembling to its rise. The twilight of the early winter morning, the piercing sweetness of the voices rising in the still air, the tune and the words she loved so well, 'Christians, awake, salute the happy morn!'

Then heaven would open.

from

The Diary of Margaret Leicester Warren (aged 15)

(Youngest daughter of the 2nd Lord de Tabley of Tabley House near Knutsford)

TABLEY, DECEMBER 1862

Monday 21st. Off to Manchester with papa. Started early in the brougham to Knutsford whence we got into the new train and arrived at about 12 to Manchester. It is a horrid day anywhere but particularly dark and smoky in the streets of Manchester wh. is generally gloomy, as we walked through them to the Star Hotel, here we lunched on pink chops and beer and spent the aft. in shopping which was rather fun. There were shawls and knives to be chosen for the school children, bonbons for the Xmas dinner and presents for everyone. The shops looked so pretty with their Xmas decorations, particularly a fruit market, piles of shining apples and oranges ornamented with holly and the cielings (*sic*) hung with festoons of evergreens and miseltoe, but the prettiest thing of all was the German fair, stalls of toys at 1d each and at 1 end of the building was a large frosted Xmas tree, hung with toys and standing on a glacier on which were scattered Swiss cottages and little goatherds and

sheperdess, then there was a sort of peep show called 'the fairy tavern' all gold stalactites and swans swimming, a looking glass and another very similar called the 'hermits cave' . . . well after the German fair we went to some more shops, bought prizes for the Xmas Tree and got to Altringham about 4 where we had a cold fly drive home.

Tuesday 23rd. Worked at Xmas decoration all morning, wrote to Meriel.

Wednesday 24th. Xmas eve. I repaired to the chapel where we spent nearly the whole day. In the evening there were waits as usual and *whist*! Such a way of spending Xmas eve!

Xmas Day – dear Meriel, how different her and Allen's quiet Xmas together must be to this and how strange it is not to have her here – the first Xmas that we have spent apart. How one misses her and how often one mentally wishes them happy returns of this day. O may every one they spend together in her new home be happier! Every new year begin with brighter hopes! I need not say how disappointed I am that they are not there. Well, this morning papa gave me a photoph. book, Nel a box of chocolate, brother 2 prints and old Mr B an Almanack for 1863. Such a lovely Xmas day, more like Australia than England, the sun poured in thro' the chapel window behind the reading desk and lit up the east end. Only Mr W and Mr B to lunch, and the evening ended in a beautiful red sunset wh. brother and I took a walk to look at and were joined by Mr Bathurst. Dinnertime. Dinnertime came and with it the Hills and Walkers. Mr Walker took me in – sat between him and Minny and wore holly berries and best gown. When the Commerce was over at which I won a photo frame, Mr B expressed a wish to see the servants dancing so he, Mama, I and the other guests trooped down

the passage to the servants hall. It was hung with evergreens and dimly lit and everyone stopped dancing as we entered. Go on, said Mama, and in vain William fluted, till at length Wilkinson led Miss H to the top of the hall, the other couples formed, and we went down one dance together, I dancing with Mr Bathurst, and very amusing it was, and so ended Xmas day 1862.

Wednesday 31st. A lovely morning. Wrote to Allen. The passing bell is ringing the old year goodnight! goodnight! what I wd. give to hear her sing that tonight.

Jan. 1st 1863. We did not see the old year out last night, at least I was in bed when 1863 came in – today has been rather eventful. 1st there was my lesson with Mr Walker, then church to which Miss Swinton and Bathurst came, besides papa, Nel and myself. The afternoon poured with rain. Sister went to Knutsford and Nel and Mr Bathurst and I, having a vain attempt to get a walk, gave it up and set out glass in the billiard room. This mg. I heard from Amy Lascelles. Well tonight the Holmes and Cooks came to dinner. I dined, took in Mr Holmes and sat between Mr S and Mrs Cook. After dinner Mrs Walker and 3 children, the Hills and 6 Clowes trouped in. At about 9 o'clock music struck up and we danced till about 12. It was rather fun but it is not worth writing much about it.

Christmas at Thornton Manor

The extremely successful pantomimes given each year by the Port Sunlight Players at the Gladstone Hall in the village recall the first incursion of dramatic art into the Lever regime – the Manor Mummers.

This 'company' was under the presidency of Mr William Hesketh Lever, the first Lord Leverhulme, and largely a family affair. Its aim, in addition to creating interest among the members themselves was to provide Christmas entertainment for the staff and tenants on the Estate. Mr Hulme Lever, who later became the second lord, was a prime mover in the effort and took character parts in all the productions.

The whole arrangement to start with was very light-hearted and the early programmes, which proclaimed the shows as taking place at 'Joyville Theatre,' Thornton Manor, were all set out in humorous vein.

Thus we find that the sole lessee and manager is Mr W.H. Lever, but the 'Actual Manager' is Mrs Lever while Miss Green is the 'General Factotum.' The booking-office, we are told, is 'opened and shut daily' and there is an announcement that good children are admitted at half-price. Seats are quoted as 'worth a guinea a box' and a foot-note requests patrons not to throw bricks at the players. 'Advertisements' appearing around the main text are in the same key.

– H.A. Robinson
Cheshire Life

HI! YOU CAN'T AFFORD
TO LOSE ANY SUNLIGHT THIS WEATHER

William Lever (1st Viscount Leverhulme) made full use of the
seasons to advertise his Sunlight soap

No account of my father's private and family life would be
complete without a reference to his Christmas house-parties at
Thornton Manor. As the house grew in size, so did these
gatherings become larger, and on Christmas Day it was
seldom fewer than fifty people – sisters, nephews and neices,
their families, close personal friends, old friends of early days
and their families – sat down to Christmas dinner, carried
through with old-time ritual. On Christmas Eve the family,
the guests and the domestic staff invariably assembled in the
music-room to hear my father read Dicken's *A Christmas
Carol*, which he knew almost by heart, and considered the
finest sermon in the English language. He used to read from a
copy of the abridged version which Dickens himself used for
his public readings. After Christmas came amateur theatricals.
To encourage my enthusiasm in this direction, my father built
a stage in the ball-room at Thornton Manor, and starting –
almost inevitably – with H.J. Byron's *Our Boys*, thirteen plays

in all have been given at Christmas time by an amateur company composed of members of the family and friends, called – the name was my father's own choice – 'The Manor Mummers'.

from *VISCOUNT LEVERHULME*
by his Son

Lines On
New Year's Day

FERDINANDO JACKSON

*Not everyone, it seems, rises to the challenge of a new year
with hope and great expectation. Ferdinando Jackson of
Rainow near Macclesfield, writing in 1829, saw it quite
differently.*

Still with unabated speed,
Hours, and days, and months proceed;
Time, that power whom all obey,
Rushes forward night and day:
Round and round this ponderous earth,
Keeps the motion from its birth;
And those heavens above us roll,
Subject not to man's controul.
He, poor creature of a day,

A Cheshire Christmas

Flourishes and fades away.
How can he contend with time?
Soon is past his glowing prime.
Soon his mortal hour comes on,
When the blusterer must be gone.
Finished is another year,
What avails the falling tear.
For our friends and kindred flown,
Mighty death! thy power we own.
While twelve months have run their round,
Cold and silent in the ground,
Thousands lie, no more they know
Of life, with all its load of woe;
Many a cheek lies wan and pale;
What can rosy health avail?

When the great destroyer calls,
If he strikes, the victim falls;
Dress the future as you please,
Call for pleasures, health and ease,
Let the flowery landscape rise,
Charming to the youthful eyes;
Then expect some sudden stroke,
Coming like an earthquake's shock:
Or the rushing whirlwind's blast,
Bliss on earth can never last;
What the future year may bring,
Earth, we know, will own the spring;
Winter, with his sullen gloom,
Cannot brook the sweet perfume,
Wafted from the springing flowers,
Nurs'd by gently falling showers.
Yon bright sun shall glow again,
And the daisies strew the plain;

But frail man must pass away,
Hungry death will seek his prey.
Numbers lie in his cold arms,
Ere bright summer lose her charms.
Let the thoughtless, giddy throng,
Mad and careless, pass along;
Not for ever can they stay,
Time will sweep them all away.

from

Twixt Mersey and Dee

HILDA GAMLIN

*Published in 1897, Mrs Gamlin's fascinating anecdotal
guide was inspired, she wrote in her Preface, 'by the easy
access to outlying villages in the peninsula of Wirral afforded
by the new lines of railway . . . and it might make an
afternoon's outing more agreeable if a book were put together
showing the principal features worthy of inspection . . .
interspersed with local histories, antiquities, etc, and remarks
upon some of the more interesting persons who may have dwelt
therein'.*

145

Old-fashioned customs still find observance in Neston. The New Year is awaited by assembling at the public cross at midnight, and singing the doxology. For thirty-seven years the same hymn has been sung as the clock strikes the Old Year out and the New Year in – 'Jesus shall reign where'er the sun'.

Quite a different mode of seeing the Old Year out is observed in the Mersey district. Large numbers of persons usually cross the river to Liverpool to pass the time until 11.45 p.m., when the last boat of the year sets off from Liverpool, crowded with passengers, who are not landed at Seacombe until the New Year is in. They cruise about mid-river until the clock in the ferry tower knells that the Old Year has gone. As the last stroke ceases, a cheer of welcome to the New Year resounds; the whistle blows furiously, adding to the varied diabolical Brocken-like discord, that screeches and hoots in prolonged revelry.

New Year's Day

(Air – 'Auld Lang Syne')

WILLIAM TAYLOR

When it comes to singing 'Auld Lang Syne' as the New Year dawns, anyone not born north of the border has to resort to la-la-ing the tune while any Scots present insist on displaying their superior knowledge by going on to the second and subsequent verses – usually in a much louder voice. But in 1866 a certain William Taylor, poet of Macclesfield, wrote an alternative version – in plain English – for the Sassenachs.

Though dark and drear has been the year
Through which we all have past;
In gloomy care or sad despair
Our days have run to waste:

CHORUS
But let this day, this New Year's Day
Be bright with love and peace;
Let joys abound the earth around,
And sin and sorrow cease!

Though trade and art fail to impart
Success, our hearts to cheer:
Though wars prevail, or woes assail,
We'll never yield to fear.
Then let this day, etc

147

Though hearts below may cease to glow,
To ease our earthly lot;
Though friendship fail, or cease to hail,
Remember, God does not!
Then let this day, etc

In grief and pain may hope remain
To dry the flowing tear;
Though health may fade, or death invade,
Our God is always near.
Then let this day, etc

Acknowledgements

Special thanks are due to Joan Leach (President of The Gaskell Society) of Knutsford, Kate Atkinson (Education Officer, Lyme Park), Kenneth Oultram (President of The Randolph Caldecott Society) of Northwich, Arthur Brack of Edinburgh, the Rt Revd Ronald Brown, former Bishop of Birkenhead, the Editor and Proprietors of *Cheshire Life* magazine and the staff of the Central Library, Birkenhead.

'From the Moment the Turkeys Arrive' is published by permission of the author. 'Run-up to Christmas' was first broadcast on BBC Radio Merseyside and is reprinted by permission of the author. The extract from *Green and Pleasant Land* (Allen & Unwin 1983) is reprinted by permission of the author. 'All on Twopence a Week' was first published in *Cheshire Life*, December 1980, and is reprinted with acknowledgement to the copyright holder. The extract from *The Christmas Book* (Robert Hale 1984) is reprinted by permission of the author. 'The Donkey's Tale' and 'Festive Initiation' are reprinted by permission of the author. 'The Peace Problem' was first published in *Cheshire Life*, December 1934, and is reprinted with acknowledgement to the copyright holder. 'Christmas Greetings' was first published in 1886 in *Alice's Adventures Under Ground*. The two extracts from *Treasure on Earth* are reprinted by permission of the administrators of Lyme Park and Stockport Metropolitan Borough Council. 'A Christmas Meditation' was first published in *The Vanishing Roads and Other Essays* (G.P. Puttnam's Sons, New York, 1915). 'Christmas Storms and

Sunshine' was first published in *Howitt's Journal*, 1848. 'An Old Cheshire Christmas' was first published in *Cheshire Life*, December 1963, and is reproduced with acknowledgement to the copyright holder. The extracts from *Thelwell's Brat Race* (Eyre Methuen 1977) are published by permission of the author. 'Stick-in-the-Mud' was first published in *Cheshire Life*, January 1959, and is reprinted with acknowledgement to the copyright holder. 'The Scribe's Tale' is published by permission of the author. 'Women's Christmas Lunch' was first published in *The Sheltering Coast* (National Poetry Guild 1992) and is reproduced by permission of the author. 'The Christmas Ghost of Poulton Lancelyn' was first published in *Cheshire Life*, 1950, and is reprinted with acknowledgement to the copyright holder. 'Christmas at Lyme' was first published in *Cheshire Life*, December 1961, and is reprinted by permission of William Bromley Davenport Esq. The extracts from *Bishop's Brew* (Arthur James 1991) are reprinted by permission of the compiler. 'A Christmas Carol' and 'Christmas-Easter' were first published in *Homage to Cheshire* (The Independent Press, now The United Reform Church in the United Kingdom) and are reprinted with their permission. The newspaper extract in 'A-beagling We Will Go!' is taken from the *Heswall and Neston News*, 1 January 1977, and is reprinted by permission of The Wirral News Group.

All unattributed items are by Alan Brack.

Picture Credits

Pages 5, 10, 60, 70, 84, 87, 94, 97, 99, 135 – *Cheshire Life* Picture Library. Page 22 – the Governors of Chetham's Library, Manchester. Page 27 – Dean and Chapter of Chester Cathedral. Pages 39, 40 – (from glass negatives of photographs taken by the butler, Truelove) Administrators of Lyme Hall. Pages 42, 44 – Mrs Judith Clegg, Gawsworth. Page 50 – private donor. Page 91 – Birkenhead Central Library. Pages 111, 114 – Mrs June Lancelyn Green, Poulton Lancelyn. Page 130 – the late W. Victor Smith Esq, Caldy. Page 142 – Port Sunlight Heritage Centre.